VALEDICTORIAN

TANVISHA NANDAN

Made with ♥ on the Notion Press Platform
www.notionpress.com

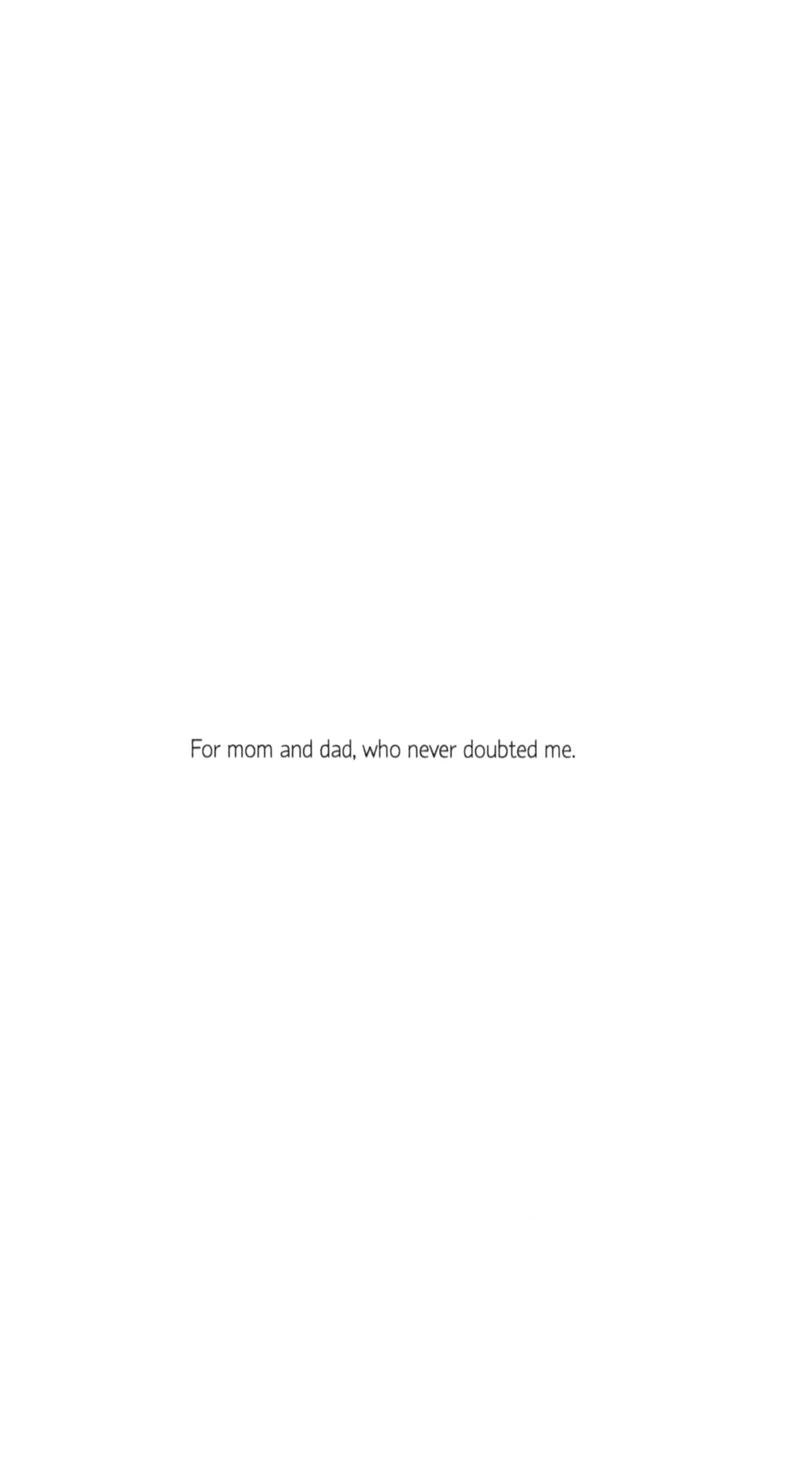

For mom and dad, who never doubted me.

Contents

1. 1   1

2. 2   27

3. 3   51

4. 4   74

5. 5   94

6. 6   104

7. 7   125

Part 1

8. 8   133

1

I didn't know if there were other reasons, but some special ones made my summers always joyful at the beginning and anxious at the end. If it weren't for all the fame and respect I had among my teachers, relatives, parents and some of my good friends, I could have suffered more than I think or even imagine. Maybe, it'll sound a little exaggerating but it's true. People think first rankers have nothing to worry about, but this perception penetrates deep into the concise of one such ranker, and then, they force themselves to dwell in that artificial pot of being the ideal student, forgetting their own perceptions and accepting the norms of the society. It can hurt some, for these things actually matter to them. Such rankers may think it's important, but maybe it's not. At least, that's what I tried to think but failed.

The light splashed on my face like a bucket of water and I turned to my side to avoid it, but my mother shook me up. It was the last day of school before the vacations started, but there was something special in our trip. Mummy was going to Pune with papa and granddad for her check-up, and her train was due for almost midnight. She wasn't going to take me with her, as I had to stay and study, and even I didn't want a ride outside for the first time in a while.

It seemed as if I'd lost interest in travelling, but I realized I didn't have enough time to mesmerize my eyes with the beauty of the city. So it was better to focus on the exams going to be held after the vacations.

She shouted from the kitchen after waking me up completely, while I laid on my bed, looking up at the ceiling and feeling my muscles, as if self-scanning myself like a robot. I still felt tired, as if my muscles had worked the whole night. The thought of taking some rest was dismissed nonetheless. I thought it would be alright after my meeting with friends at school but then on the other hand, I didn't want to go because of the two continuous mathematics period. The one thing I hated. And moreover, seeing the holiday so close, any student wished it to be holiday even on the last working day. And I was one of them; I didn't care what was being taught on the last day, most of the students dared to stay at home, declaring their own holidays. Sadly, I couldn't do the same.

I folded the bed sheets and proceeded towards the living room, rubbing my eyes to show my parents I wanted to sleep. Well, that trick never worked on my mother, but my father always consoled that he would let me sleep till late morning during the holidays and not let mummy wake me up. My elder sisters wouldn't bother to wake me up, but when mother would instruct Tarini the eldest among us, she would either call out so softly on purpose so that she could report my ignorance to my mother or shout in my ear. Then we would end up fighting with pillows and getting scolded for creating a ruckus early in the morning. But that day, she decided not to do that, since she had some event in her college and was busy preparing for it, rather than disturbing her younger sister.

'How does this look?' she asked me, showing her maroon saree to me as I entered the room again to find her. My sister was beautiful, even if she didn't wear all the ornaments and the fancy dresses she bought. Her skin glowed bright all the time, and her long brown hair seemed like a waterfall of honey when they were let down. But still, what answer would you expect from a notorious little sister?

'Ugh! Did you just get out of a gutter?' I replied, dramatically pinching my nose and making a face. Tarini sighed and narrowed her brown, kohl-lined eyes at me as I burst into laughter.

'What can I even expect from a little monster like you,' she spat and giggled herself, looking at the mirror and adjusting her hair clips. 'Now you better get ready, papa won't drop us today.'

'Then who will? I'm not going with you, I've to live long enough to become something,' I asked, and she nearly swatted me with her comb. I laughed again and this brought mother to our room. She scowled, looking at the hundred dresses lined up outside the closet; except they were in a mess. This reminded me of Wanda Petronski from 'The Hundred Dresses'. Except, my sister wasn't shy like her.

'I thought you selected your event dress beforehand?' she retorted. 'What is all this mess? I clean up the house and then there are four people who don't care what they do!'

'I keep my things in place!' I protested and I saw father peeping from the doorway, with a shaver in his hand and a towel on his bare shoulder.

'Even I do,' he said, and mother turned to look at him but he disappeared. She turned to take our class there.

'Clean this before you leave,' she instructed. 'And Tara, help your sister before you get ready.'

'Why should I help her? This is not even my room!' I whined but seeing the look in my mother's eyes, I understood I should keep quiet. Nobody had the fantasy of getting slapped in the morning. Even though that had stopped for a year, I still feared it.

'Because you can, and it'll not take much time,' she said and left the room. I turned to Tarini who frowned, looking down at her mobile phone.

'No wonder you grab that thing of yours so fast,' I muttered and began stashing her clothes in the closet. I realized I only had some clothes, since I didn't like shopping much for those things, and books were my top priority when somebody asked me about my wish list (which no one did). I had three pairs of jeans, two black tops and two baggy pants mother ordered online for me. But Tarini had an ocean of several dresses, most of them being traditional. Even I had some, and most of the time I preferred wearing them, but now that I had bought baggy jeans which were in fashion recently, I wore them mostly.

'Will you visit the event with me? After school?' Tarini asked, looking up at me.

'I've to go to a place called school,' I snapped at her. 'And I'm not in a mood to leave my meetings.'

'I mean, after the school ends,' my elder sister said, her eyes glittering. 'I'll pick you up after school and we shall enjoy the fair there.'

'Won't your friends be queasy about it?' I asked, rather annoyed. I didn't enjoy much while being with Tarini's female friends, but her all boy friends were sure fun, since they were literally a copy of my friends. And I knew she wouldn't hang out with them then.

'Oh no they'll rather enjoy your company,' Tarini waved away my question. 'Remember Sameer? He's joining us too. The last time when he came over, you enjoyed your time with him. I bet you'll enjoy this time as well.'

'Oh, Sameer's good,' I agreed. 'But I don't want to interfere in your free time. Wouldn't he be... uneasy for that?'

'Oh he likes spending time with you, just like his little sister,' she replied, stuffing her lipstick in her sling bag. 'And moreover, his brother would come too, and he's your age. Likes Roblox, mangas, dragons, and-'

'I *hate* him,' I snorted.

'But you haven't even met him yet!'

'Nah! I'd still hate him.'

'You're such a big introvert!'

'Thanks!'

She busied herself with texting someone, and I cleaned up the closet. If I went out with her, maybe I could have a good time eating stuff around made by the college students. Last year, it'd been the best time for me. I'd enjoyed with Sameer playing arcade games installed for the fair only, and we even sang some songs in the Japanese Culture section. Last year had been totally banger.

'What's the theme for this year?' I asked Tarini.

'Traditional,' she replied, pretending to not care much about my questions. 'This year's fair is going to be interesting as well! Trust me!'

'Okay then, but will I be in my school uniform only?'

'We won't have time to get home, and if you do, mom will catch you and won't let you go with me.'

'Convince her then,' I said finally, narrowing my eyes at her. 'I'm not taking the responsibility, *you* are. And you should be the one to-'

'FINE, Ms Discipline!' Tarini growled, rolling her eyes. I'd a great insult for that as well, but I decided to get the great feast and then taunt her for that gesture. She stomped out of the room and I followed behind, pretending to busy myself in brushing the teeth.

'Ma, I'm taking Tara to the Annual fair today,' I heard her say to our mother in kitchen. 'I'll pick her up after school.'

'What? No need for that!'

I flinched myself when I heard the scolding. I was already expecting that to happen, since my mother never allowed me for such parties and gatherings. I'd never opposed the idea, because I was an ambivert myself and I never had liked going out in midst of a crowd. It always made me nervous and anxious and much more cautious even if it was just a safe place. It made me tired, to say the least.

But this was another situation, where I *was* willing to go somewhere. And the chances of my mother approving it was point one percent.

'I'm not leaving her with your *male* friends!' my mother snapped at Tarini. I peeked from behind the door, my mouth foaming with the mint flavoured Pepsodent paste. 'If only there is Amaya!'

'Amaya will be there with me all the time ma,' Tarini said at length. 'She doesn't leave my side and Tara's in class twelve now. She's matured enough to not leave my side.'

This was a plus point of having elder siblings, for me at least. Tarini always supported me wherever I was right, or where our mother misinterpreted things which were simple as ice. Though we never stopped fighting or pulling each other's legs, we were still one soul. I hid their secrets and they hid mine.

I smiled secretly and the saliva filled with paste dripped from the mouth. Yuck.

'I'll take care of her,' Tarini pleaded. 'Please ma?'

There was moment of silence which made my heart leap. It was the moment of time which would lead to my sadness for the whole day or the joy for holidays. I realized I was actually wanting to go to the fair.

'Okay, take her, but don't you dare leave her alone with *any* friend, be it your best friend or worst,' my mother instructed her and I leapt with joy. My father watched me curiously as I cleaned my mouth and ran to the kitchen. Tarini nodded at ma and just when she turned, she almost got surprised.

'There, there, don't hop like a bunny now,' she said, smiling at me and heading to her room. 'Get ready for school dumbo.'

I obediently took a bath and got into my school uniform quickly to have the breakfast at the table with my family. The maid who cleaned the house had been dismissed for the time being, since my mother was anxious to leave the two of us with some stranger, even if that stranger had been working for a year now. I didn't have any problem with it. Moreover, it was a joy that I would have some quality time for myself.

As I feasted on the muesli, I noticed how Tarini was struggling with the short bangs of her hair and almost ate her hair while taking a spoonful of muesli in her mouth. She growled at times to herself while we watched the news as the morning ritual. I paid much more attention on planning out what I was going to wear. I'd baggy jeans and a black shirt which did well with the black jeans, and even a matching clip bow. Or I could even wear the long grey pleated skirt and black top with shallow heels. But that would look too much. It was Tarini's event, not mine. I was just going to feast on the tasty food items and buy a stuff or two which the students made with their own hands.

'Till when will you two be back home?' father asked, looking at Tarini specifically. 'You know we've our train at midnight.'

'It won't take time, we'll be back by seven,' Tarini said. She looked around the table, searching for someone, and even I realized that someone was missing.

'Where's Ava?' she asked, chewing on the flakes.

'Oh, she said she'd some early classes today, so she left,' our mother told us. 'She'll be back early, don't worry.'

Ava, the middle child, not neglected as some said about middle children but not overly cared about as well. Mother and father were neutral about her and Tarini, but they weren't going to leave me neutral, for some reason. Maybe because I topped the class and scored better than most of them. Or at least, I did the *job*.

I reached school and took my seat to attend the last class of the month. It was a half day, and there was much excitement about the plans for the vacations among the students of my class.

'Hey Tara, where are you going this summer?' Prasanna, my best friend, asked me.

'Nowhere,' I replied, doodling an eye on the empty pages of my scrap diary. It was a free period, and most of them were doing nothing in the classroom except chatting with their friends. I was in the library with her but I wasn't interested in picking a book and reading too, so I decided I could pass the time away in leisure, thinking about life.

Deep thinker, eh?

'Mummy and papa are going to Pune with dadaji,' I told her. 'For some medical work, you know.'

'So this means that you're getting your own leisure time?' she bubbled, her eyes glittering as if I'd just told her the location of some hidden treasure. 'Cool! I wish I could be alone for some time too.'

'Well, you do get the whole morning and part of evening to stay alone,' I smiled, resting my chin over my left palm. 'What else do you want? And I'm totally not alone. Tarini and Ava are staying too.'

'But you three have your separate rooms,' Prasanna said. 'And you can do whatever you want with nobody to scold you.'

I shrugged my shoulders and said nothing. I knew how much of leisure I was getting.

"Study and don't do any other stuff apart from studying. This is class twelve, not a joke. I don't want you to score less than ninety six this time."

My mother's words rang in my ear again and again, echoing from the walls of my heart and coming back to slap me again. It was as if a machine was fit in me about such things. I couldn't ignore the fact that I thought myself as a robot sometimes.

OBEY

'The group is planning to go to some leisure place and have a long talk,' Prasanna said, fiddling with her pen and looking at me, as I almost folded the book page. 'Woah! You don't treat books like that! What's the matter?'

'Nothing,' I mumbled, and looked at her to avoid any sad topics to resurface again. 'Where are you guys going?'

'Don't say "you", say "we"' she snapped at me, frowning. You're grown up now, and you'll come with us. I'll convince aunty if required. You're coming with us.'

'Who all are there?'

'Shashank, and his friend fatso.'

'Ugh! Not *him*!' I protested, whispering so that the librarian doesn't throw us out. 'I'd rather study then than listen to his trash talks! Isn't Neera coming?'

'If you want her to come, we can invite her too,' Prasanna smirked and I tried to hide my blush with an angry face and narrowed eyes. 'Is the great valedictorian of all time blushing at the name of a regular classmate she has?'

She peeked at me and I snarled at her, finally breaking into an uncontrollable smile. But, fortunately or unfortunately, I didn't know how to term this, Neera came right to our table with her Mathematics textbook and a diary, sitting beside me.

'Hey! Can you help me with some problems?' she asked cheerfully, and I was so embarrassed, I thought she could see my blush. I nodded quickly and took out my handkerchief rapidly in the pretext of wiping my face. But Prasanna's evil grin caught me off-guard and I smiled at her goofy grin.

I'll catch you later, I said to her with my eyes.

We'll see, she winked back and dropped her gaze to her book. But I knew she wasn't going to read. She was keeping an intense look at us from the corner of her eye like a spy. I couldn't help the fact that whenever I saw Neera, my heart leapt like fire and while alone with my thoughts, it burnt with flames of mingled feelings and confusion. Was it only attraction, which occurred when you got a true friend? But it didn't happen to me even once when I was with Prasanna. These thoughts always washed me ashore whenever I tried to find an answer.

'Did you doze off with your eyes open?' Neera said, looking at me closely. Our faces where inches away and when I realized this, I drew back with reflex and nodded at her. She showed me her problem and I explained her how to solve it. No doubt we were best friends, but I never talked about to her beyond this. The only thing I hid inside me.

DISGRACE

'Hey Neera, will you come hang out with us on Sunday?' Prasanna opened her cursed beak again. I glared at her as Neera, who was leaned over to look at the problem and our shoulders where touching each gently, looked up at her adjusting her thin rimmed glasses. Her heat warmed my cold heart, and I stared at Prasanna indignantly.

What a great way to disturb your own best friend, my look told her everything.

'Where are you guys going?' Neera asked with great interest, a smile spreading on her fair face.

'PM Mall, if Tara agrees,' my best friend replied, resting her chin on her hand as Neera looked at me and smiled warmly. How it stole my heart away! Fortunately, the library was slightly noisy with the students of grade six working over some project at a corner, otherwise, Neera could've heard my heart beat.

'Why not? Come with us,' she said, tucking her small locks behind her ears. 'We're all free during the vacations. Let's have fun!'

I was about to say something, when Prasanna interrupted.

'We need to convince her mummy first,' she said, as if drafting a plan to rescue me. 'I wish it was easier, but maybe, you can convince her, Neera. She'd listen to you, since you've visited Tara's house a many times.'

'Of course I will,' Neera nodded. I coloured the eye with my pen while looking down and a soft grip on my wrist made me look up. The touch sent current running down my spine and goose bumps emerged on my skin. Thankfully, we had full sleeved shirts in class twelfth. Saving me from embarrassment.

'But my parents are going out of town this summer,' I told the two of them, to avoid turning red like a tomato. 'How'll you talk to mummy?'

'That's not a problem, it made the solution much easier,' Prasanna waved her hand. 'We can talk over the phone. And let the two of us draft a plan for it. You just get the right outfit to go out.'

'Sure.'

I kept my left hand on my thigh and continued sketching the eye I'd drawn. It kind of reminded me about the eye I'd always seen in my dreams, and maybe, it was the one I was sketching unconsciously. The eyes that were always on me. The eyes that always stared. I thought I could write a poem on it. It'd been long since I'd written one. Only because my parents thought writing couldn't earn someone money.

'Writing? As a career?' my mother looked at me from her mobile phone with a frown on her face.

I was too afraid to say anything, so I just looked down at the marbled floor, trying to find something interesting. Maybe, I shouldn't have opened my mouth for it.

'Tara, you know you aren't going to earn anything in that,' my father spoke. 'That's just ridiculous. You didn't get the first

rank to get into writing?'

'But it's not a bad job, I write nicely, and I even got my story published in the biggest children magazine,' I protested now, anger filling in me. They could say anything about me, but not about my passion. Writing was my first love. 'You can see the potential there and yet you don't believe me!'

'Don't shout here!' my mother yelled. I began breathing heavily with the rage that was habitually making space in me, but knowing I couldn't yell further and just insult myself, it added as a fuel. Plus, I wasn't keen on getting slapped again. 'We know what's best for you and not you! You're not our parents! And you will follow what we say!'

'But it's my life!' I said again. My cursed mouth won't stop counter attacking.

Because I know what's right for me, and not them.

'I want to be a writer,' I tried to explain, controlling my tears. 'What's wrong in that? Haven't you seen so many famous writers? Do you doubt me?'

'Yes we do,' my father scowled. 'Writing is not a career. It's just waste of time, and we don't want you to sit with hundred loans on your head, just like Anuj.'

'He's not in loan, for your information,' I answered. 'He's a Youtuber, and nowadays, Youtubers have much more respect than twenty four and six workers.'

'What's all this noise?' Ava came out of her room, frowning. She did know what was happening; she knew everything. But she still walked to me and looked at mother and father on the edge of killing me for arguing.

'Go back to your room, Ava,' my mother said slowly, fixing her gaze at me. 'You don't need to get involved.'

'Why? Was I brought from a garbage bin?' Ava said in the calmest voice, as she always did, and my father got up, looking at her. This was turning violent. And it was all my fault. 'Fine,

I'm going. But please reconsider your choices. You're only digging traps for your old age, because Tara is the only one who'll continue to work-'

'GET OUT OF HERE!' *my mother shouted and I flinched, clutching at Ava's hoodie. But my sister remained nonchalant. She sighed and walked back into her room, and I looked down again.*

'We really don't expect anything from you now, Tara,' *mother shook her head slowly, her voice cracking.*

You made her cry. You're a disgrace.

'Just go away from here,' *my father said, slumping back into the sofa. 'Get out of here. We don't expect you to look after us.'*

I sighed heavily, totally lost into my own world. The noise had blurred around me, as if my ears had been cushioned to listen only to my intrusive thoughts and overthink. As I always did. Everything was a past now, and they even said it in a calmer way afterwards that they wanted what's best for me. They even apologised for their words.

I understood their feelings. They just wanted what was best for me.

'Lost somewhere?' Neera shook me to reality. I looked at her and said I was just thinking something.

'You hide so many things from me,' she whispered, solving a maths sum. I could see a few mistakes in her steps but I didn't interrupt. 'But I respect that. It's okay if you don't want to tell me. But I can tell that something's been bothering you.'

'You've been saying that to me since class eight,' I smirked, resting my chin on my left hand and scribbling other eyes around the great eye I'd drawn. 'What about you?'

'What about me?'

'All things about you.'

'All things about me? Like bother?'

'No, my medicine.'

I could see her grin without even taking my eyes off my drawing. I knew Prasanna was enjoying this scene, but I was too tired to hide my redness now. It calmed me from my thoughts. Neera silenced the storm brewing inside me. Always. She was my medicine absolutely.

'Stop flirting in the library, idiot,' she said, and I glanced at her hot red cheeks. She didn't look at me, but I could clearly see she was making more mistakes than focusing.

'That's wrong,' I pointed and she hit my hand lightly. 'Hey! What did I do?'

'Shush!' she snarled and looked back at her notebook. I finally matched my gaze with my best friend, who was busy watching the scenery.

Good going, she smiled widely.

Thank you, I winked back.

After the school ended shortly, I walked back to the same spot where I waited for my sister to pick me up for the event. It was near the big banyan tree near the school, and even though the whole road was covered from the harsh rays because of the pleasant canopy of trees that casted celadon crystals down from the leaf gaps, this tree was noticeably huge and old, like it was the leader of the gang. I particularly loved summer and winter, then came monsoon and lastly, spring and autumn. Each season dictated how the mood of an individual can change with season, and so can the thoughts. I wondered why mine rarely did that.

As I waited, I saw Neera waving at me and sprinted towards me. When we stood together, she was slightly taller than me in height. That made me comfortable whenever she gave me hugs at my house. And for the first time in my life, I wanted to always stay slightly shorter than her. Only her.

What a weird fetish you have.

'I made something for you but forgot to give it during class hours,' she said with glee and fished out from her pocket, a braided bracelet. The bracelet had shiny black stones fixed in place and a black eye pendant as a charm. Neera knew I liked black items. And she made something for me.

I won't lie, but it did touch my heart more than a best friend's gift should have.

'Do you like it?' she asked, keeping her hands at the back and peeking at my face. I examined the bracelet with great care and wore it immediately.

'I love it,' I said and a wide smile spread over her face. 'You clearly knew why you placed an eye charm, didn't you?'

'I know your choices and fetishes,' Neera winked at me. 'I enchanted this charm to protect you from the eyes in your dreams. A shield, for instance.'

'Oh really?' I guffawed. Neera tucked her bangs and looked down with a smile. For a moment, we didn't talk, and I was wondering what else I could say to keep the conversation alive.

'I'm glad you liked it,' she said at last, looking up. Her cheeks were red as a ray of sunlight fell on them, and lighted up her brown eyes. I could never have removed my gaze from them, had my sister's scooty didn't come beside me.

'God, I thought you came from the back gate?' Ava grumbled, taking off her helmet and peering at us. I stammered for a second, thinking she must have noticed the three second eye gaze of ours, but honestly, those seconds felt like years. Years I could look into them without withering away.

'No, I always come out from the front gates,' I replied. Ava took a look at Neera, who greeted her politely and her expressions softened. She was dressed in black shirt and pants, as she usually wore, and her long black hair was let down behind her, almost touching the leather seat. Her kohl lined eyes looked at Neera with great interest, even though she'd met her before, and I was hoping she hadn't guessed it out. Ava knew much more about the LGBTQ community because of her internet knowledge. Luckily, she was neutral and never hated them.

'Come, hop on the seat,' she said. I turned to face Neera quickly, as if I was leaving her forever.

'Give me a call when you guys decide the plan,' she said, holding my hands, and for the first time, I wished her to not, at least in front of Ava. I wasn't ready yet to tell any of my sisters about it, let alone my parents. But the soft touch prevented me from breaking away.

I nodded at her and she smiled, running her hand through the bracelet I was wearing. Ava watched silently as Neera waved me goodbye and I was absorbed in watching her go until she had become one with the crowd of students.

'Girlfriend?' Ava said in her calmest voice, as if nothing was new to her and she'd been knowing it for too long. I sighed and supported myself up the scooty, keeping a hand on her shoulder and resting my forehead on her back.

'Tell me, I won't tell anyone, not even Tarini,' Ava urged again as she started the scooty and drove away from the noise of the school. Soon, the tree canopy was out and the harsh rays fell on us, heating up my hair. I fiddled with the bracelet, thinking if Ava should really know about this.

I'm just as disgraceful as a child not getting good marks.

'None of your business, nosy,' I snapped at her. 'I don't want to talk about it right now. And where were you this morning?'

'Changing the topic?' Ava asked, and I could feel her smirking. 'That's none of your business too.'

'Whatever.'

I was lost deep in my own thoughts about the event, now that Neera had finally decided to leave my mind for some minutes.

'Are you coming with us to the event too?' I asked Ava.

'Nah, I've lots of assignments to complete,' she replied, snorting. 'I better complete them. Don't want to be scolded by the teacher.'

I looked up at the traffic ahead, as my back began burning with the scorching rays. It was the first week of May, and the summer heat was already taking form. Global warming could've been one cause, but anyways, I liked summer. The vibes of my childhood it gave off were precious for me, and I tried to make each summer better. But most probably, this one wasn't going to be any better.

'How will you even tell mom and dad about it?' Ava spoke suddenly. I couldn't have heard it in the speed, but when she slowed down due to traffic, we began talking. I wasn't very close to Ava, but we sure did share secrets with each other; at least, I did. And I knew she wasn't going to spill it anywhere. 'I mean, if this is serious.'

'Everything I take is serious,' I said. 'At least, in these kind of matters. I can't help it.'

'I know, and for your information, I don't hate you,' she said roughly. 'I know you've responsibilities, because mom and dad don't have it for me. I can't be a people pleaser for them.'

'Hmm.'

We stopped near an ice-cream parlour. This was not what I'd expected, but I could go with a Belgian chocolate tri-cone at that hour. It was almost twelve. Ava asked me to stay in the shade of the shop and after some time, came out of the shop with two chocolate cones. We shared the same flavour of ice-cream, and I actually had someone who didn't hate chocolate flavour in my family. I peeled open the wrapper and got to work. Amidst the heat and the sweat, the ice-cream tasted way better and provided some relief.

'So you're bisexual?' Ava asked, focusing on her cone. I nodded. I'd thought a lot about it. So much that I'd got a headache. Not that I hated myself, because if God had intended me to be this way, I'd no right to be mad at him because I hadn't done any crime. I loved myself the way I was. But mom and dad weren't going to like this. Not at all. *I still have college and job to do. Better not focus on these things.*

'No problem,' Ava said, and I glanced at her, while a drop of chocolate trickled down to my thumb. I licked it after seeing that nobody was watching us. 'You know, people have made this a stone written fact that only a boy and girl can fall in love. It's not the gender that really matters, in my opinion. What do you say? Is this how you feel too?'

'Yup, I do,' I replied. 'But who'll understand this? Our constitution recognises this but it's like, people of the LGBTQ community are still criminals for not loving their opposite gender, or for not being the ideal man or woman. I hate this so much.'

'Doesn't matter,' Ava shrugged her shoulders. 'I wouldn't have given a fuck if any aunty would've tried to open her faggot mouth and speak trash about my girlfriend.'

I broke into giggles and she smiled.

'No really, that's what I think too,' I said after I controlled myself. The ice cream was melting fast, so I ate it faster. 'I don't care what people think about me in these situations, because I know I haven't done any crime by loving someone of the same gender.'

'Exactly. That's how I want you to be. So does Neera know this?'

'I haven't told her anything about how I feel. We just act like best friends who are like couples. You know, the usual friend code, but I really think she can sense this in me... I don't exactly know.'

Ava nodded slowly.

But I completely don't ignore this, a thought spiralled bitterly. *I do care when I get even one mark less than someone who got higher than me. Even if it's just one subject, I can't seem to take it out of my head.*

The fair was exotic and the decorations that had been done were excellent. The set-up totally gave out a traditional vibe, with boys wearing various shades of kurta and girls either saree or kurti or lehenga. Most of them wore lehenga itself and were busy taking selfies with their friends. The vibrant colours and the beautiful girls made me want to dress up traditionally too, since I looked like an intruder amidst them. To my relief, there were many such intruders there who must be related to their brothers and sisters and had been dragged to this event too.

Tarini got busy with her friends, who were too glad to have me in their selfies too and soon, I met Sameer too. The tall spectacled guy always had an amiable smile on his olive-complexioned face, and in the fair, he looked one who was down to the earth. His hair was slicked back and he even had his black ear tops visible. I always found such things attractive on boys who weren't ashamed to wear tops or even apply black nail polish. It looked good on them. And they were confident in themselves.

'What's up dragoness?' he asked, giving me a high five.

'The sky,' I replied and we giggled. Tarini snorted but I knew she was jealous because whenever I was with Sameer, he wouldn't care to give her much time. 'How's everything going?'

'Just like butter,' Sameer said, smiling. 'Have you seen our stall yet? You'll find really good jewellery made by Sania and Jayanti.'

'I haven't, because this dumbo is busy taking photos which she'll then post all year round,' I said as a matter-of fact and got a good thwack on my head. I turned to see Tarini narrowing her eyes at me. 'Hey! It took me time to get this bun correct! Don't ruin it!'

'Come, let's go,' Sameer said. We followed him through the chattering of the colourful crowd and chanced upon a stall filled with jewelleries of all types: necklaces, bracelets, clay bead earrings and many other things. It was a shiny heaven for stuff, and of course, there were girls selecting stuff for themselves and trying out necklaces in front of the small mirror hanging alongside the bamboo pole. Sameer waved at Sania and Jayanti who were very much busy in praising the customers to urge them to buy their stuff. I calculated that they could easily earn money if the price was fair and they continued with their buttering.

'Hi Tara!' Sania gave me her widest smile while delicately packing a pair of earrings for a customer in a small newspaper bag. I saw a ton of them kept in a cardboard box next to their feet. It was a great idea but it must've cost their time too.

'Hi, your stall looks magnificient!' I said, smiling and looking at the shiny objects. My gaze shifted from one object to another, and another. But I wasn't going to buy anything for myself.

I'll gift Neera something, for her upcoming birthday. I wish I could make something instead. But mom would never spare me a chance. Or wait... I can actually make something while she's out of the town. But I can additionally buy something for her.

I wasn't that good at clay art, nor did I have any items to glaze the clay or mould it with special moulders, so I was planning to get some beads of her favourite colour and weave her a bracelet too.

'What do you want to buy, ma'am?' Jayanti said to me politely and Sania giggled. I blushed a little and said I was still looking. My gaze went to a small sun shaped pendant, made by twisting wires and it had a golden shaped stone in between. I pointed at it and asked Sania to take it out.

'How much does this cost?'

'Only ten rupees!'

'I'll buy it then.'

I knew I was going to be buying stuff around, so I'd brought my little purse full of savings there. I did keep away some money back and only took around two hundred. More than enough for a miser like me. Just then, my phone began vibrating in my pocket. I excused myself and went behind the stall. It was mummy's call.

'Are you with Tarini?' she asked.

'Yes mummy.'

'Okay, you kids come back by six. We've to hand over some important tasks to you three so that there's no fighting and all. And the timing for the train has been changed. It'll be earlier than its original time.'

I checked my watch. 5:01 PM. As expected, I could never enjoy any evening with peace.

'But mom, Tarini has to perform a play, and she won't be back until seven,' I told her. I knew she would find a way to get *me* back, but would leave Tarini for the function.

'Fine, but I'm not leaving you till that late, now that we have a situation. I'll send Ava to pick you up at around six.'

'Okay mom.'

She cut the call and I sighed. Well, I did have my share of fun while roaming around and eating stuff with Tarini's money but I really wasn't willing to go so early. I had to though. I really didn't have any choice.

'Was it ma?' Tarini asked and I nodded. She sighed as if *she* was tired with mummy's orders and not me.

'She said that the train will arrive earlier tonight so she wants us to be home soon,' I told her. 'I'll be going home with Ava at six and you're allowed to stay because of your play.'

'What work do *we* have at home?' Tarini snorted, furrowing her brows. 'It's always a reason. Always!'

'Don't be angry now,' I said. 'You know we can't help it. Two important things are on the same day, so yeah.'

Tarini didn't say anything further and walked back to her friends. I opened my mobile and looked at the wallpaper of me and my family. I never changed it, because my mother would occasionally check my phone and go through the chats to see if I'd a boyfriend or not. She liked Neera too, but had never suspected she was my unofficial love. And I wasn't interested to let her know that. All my friends who texted me knew my phone was checked, so they didn't send absurd texts but sure did tease me sometimes by calling names. Mother was neutral every time, so it wasn't much of a problem.

INVASION

I called Neera meanwhile to keep my boredom away, since I had nothing much to do, now that Tarini was busy with her friends. But soon, she paced back to me with a boy who looked about my age and was as tall as a pole. His hair was kind of messy in an attractive way and he had spectacles on, resembling much like Sameer's brother.

'This is Vaari, Sameer's brother, and he's of your age,' Tarini introduced me to him. I just looked at his nervous smile as he greeted me and I greeted back, excusing myself for second from the call.

'Be on line and don't make any noise,' I whispered to Neera.

'Sure, bunny.'

I put the phone on speaker and pretended it to be switched off, while Neera was prepared to listen to every word.

'Both of you are introverted, eh?' Sameer called out from the stall, smiling. I smiled back but I was seriously not in the mood to be interrupted while talking to Neera.

'While you sit here, you can at least socialize,' Tarini retorted and before I could stick my tongue out at her, she trotted back to her stall.

I'll give her nicely after this.

'So how's studies going?' Vaari asked me, keeping his hands at the back and looking at the tip of his brown sneakers.

'Great,' I replied. *I don't even know what we should talk about. Is this some kind of a date? Are sisters this frank with their younger sisters in India? Well, I think mine are...*

'I've seen you with Sameer bhaiya a lot, and he seems to like you much more than me,' he laughed anxiously and I supported it, so he doesn't feel awkward. Even if it was a stranger and they were polite, I was ready not to make them feel socially awkward because I knew what it felt like.

'Sameer bhaiya's nice,' I said, nodding in agreement. I had never called Sameer, Sameer bhaiya and it sounded so weird from my mouth. The two of us were almost like classmates, but I adapted myself to the way he was talking.

We talked about certain things like games, studies, news, and what rules make schools hell. It was nice enough, and I wondered if Neera felt any jealously from him. I would be glad if she did. It would show me what she actually felt about me. Not that we told each other, but our hearts knew it very well.

'Excuse me please,' Vaari said, taking out his ringing phone and moved aside. I took my own phone, removed it from speaker and giggled to let Neera know he was gone.

'Are you done with your date yet?' she snarled and I giggled harder. 'Say something or I'll surely not pity on you beautiful face later on.'

'So you do admit that I'm prettier, isn't it?' I added fuel to her fire. 'You think I'm this open with everyone?'

'No, and I'm not interested in knowing about it too,' she retorted. 'And the girls said that we'll have a discussion about out day out tomorrow night. So you better not miss it on the pretext of studying. Or better, I'll come to your house. How's that?'

'I'll appreciate it,' I laughed. 'Bye now. I'm a very busy person unlike you.'

'Yeah I know bunny, bye.'

Talking to her made me admire the sunset even more than I'd ever did in my life.

2

I helped mummy and papa bring their suitcases to the front door. It was eight in the evening, and the train was due at half past nine. Why mom had called us was to explain the rules and regulations of being home alone while we were at it. When Tarini was back we recited her the harsher version of rules I and Ava had noted. We told she was the one going to cook every day for the two of us and she'd to clean the house as well, along with feeding our pet fish and even keep the toilet clean.

'Ok that's ridiculous!' she exhaled, looking up from her mobile phone and narrowing her eyes at both of us. Mom and dad were busy caring about when granddad was going to arrive at our place. He'd said he'd be taking a taxi, but it was quarter past eight now. And the three of us were busy watching shows on the TV in the living room. Particularly, it was Ava and Tarini who watched serials where the bride was revived from death infinite times like Sekiro and where the husband married three times, at least. In my like, I wanted to watch the national geographic or the 'Forged in Fire' where they showed the perilous knife designs, but I knew they weren't going to let me. Plus, I wasn't allowed to watch TV by mummy.

'Nothing's ridiculous, you've to do these work,' Ava said, winking at me when Tarini wasn't looking. She was posting the photos she'd clicked in the event. I was sad I couldn't watch her play but thankfully, her drama teacher had the recording clearly done. I was going to watch it later, now that she'd forwarded it to my mobile phone.

'While you two sleep? No way!' Tarini muttered. This was the first time none of the elders were staying at home with us to look after us, probably because we were all grown-ups now and my two sisters could take care of the house well. I, on the other hand, planned to stay in my room all day for the vacations, studying and writing (Writing only if my mother's warning didn't haunt my mind and made me feel guilty about myself). I hadn't left my passion, I just kept it hidden beneath my Physics textbook sometimes, whenever I heard mummy coming to my room to check on me. It was a surprise that I could recognize the footstep of each and every member living in the house clearly, thus giving me a caution of who was coming. It was an awesome power I had developed. Not to mention because of the strictness.

'He's here,' my father exclaimed and the three of us, turned from the couch to look at the taxi outside the door. An elderly man of sixties stepped out, wearing a light coloured cotton shirt and dark brown trousers. As usual, granddad had a pen in his pocket; being a retired bank official, he'd been maintaining this habit since his early ages of work. It was a formal behaviour he followed, and otherwise with us three, he was totally like a friend. The white hairs scattered on his olive face shone bright in the night light outside as he proceeded forward. Our granny wasn't going, and neither she was staying here with us, instead she'd been invited by her sister to attend the wedding of some close relative's son. So it was really the three of us.

We ran to him to touch his feet and he smiled.

'My three princesses, stay home safely, okay?' he said, as we stood age-wise in front of him like ducklings. The skin near his eyes wrinkled a little as a wide grin spread on his old face. I sensed serenity for the while he was with us, but it was time for the serenity to go. I realized I felt the same when I was with Neera.

'Now, again, listen to me,' our mother instructed and we moaned in pain, looking at each other with helpless eyes. 'Stop making faces! Tarini, your task is to check on these two time to time, and for Ava, you'll help your elder sister with cleaning and cooking. Tara, you don't need to help them, but you can *only* when you've *finished* studying. Don't keep scrolling on the mobile or play games on the laptop.'

'I don't scroll on the mobile,' I defended myself but she ignored it. I knew a casual reason had to be there to be involved in the uncommon tasks I got.

'We'll be back in a few days, so don't worry okay?' a softness spread on her face and she hugged the three of us. Okay, maybe I just took her instructions like the chains that had trapped me, but weren't those chains there to shape me? I believed those chains were necessary to shape a child and instil discipline. I didn't know what to make out of the lives of other children, ones who'd yet not decided what they were going to do in future or those who were on the wrong path. I could only think about my own life and compare that to theirs, noticing how good mine was. Maybe.

The taxi sped away with the three elders and soon diminished down the bend of the road to the main road.

Then, Tarini locked the veranda gate and came in to lock the main door. She sat down with Ava to watch their serials, and now that there was no one to stop them from binge watching series, I knew there was going to be noise even in the mid of the night. So I slipped into my room quietly and got to my daily routine which never changed.

The sun pendant was kept on my study table, hidden behind some thick volumes of Chemistry and when I lifted it, I saw the golden ball looking at me. What attracted me the most towards it was the fiery appearance of it, like the actual sun had been somehow trapped inside the wires covering it. I lifted it up to get a better view and in the room light, it glistened excellently. My heart beat rapidly, thinking about the scene when I'd give it to Neera secretly in her bedroom, far from the noise of the birthday party. How glad she would be! I hadn't thought about any handmade gifts yet, but thinking about his one gave me goose bumps and I giggled to myself. Keeping the necklace inside the drawer in the envelope, I got to actually studying.

What I'd thought was true. The two couch potatoes were sleeping on the sofa, with Ava's head rested on the arm rest and Tarini on her belly. They slept like two lovers; the cushions had been kicked down and the remote was lying on the carpet below where Ava's hand was lifeless. There were some crumbs of chips on the carpet and a glass bowl was almost devoid of the popcorns they'd been eating while watching their favourite thriller series. I sighed as I took the bowl and the chips packet, collecting the bigger crumbs and switched off the TV that was now picturing the scenic beauty of the hills of Darjeeling. It was one of the many pictures that was displayed when the film was paused for a long time, and kept changing in minutes. I grabbed a blanket from my room which I wasn't going to use since it was hot, and spread it over the two of them. They were snoring softly, as if nothing was going to disturb them. I let them be and paced towards the kitchen silently, switching on the chimney light near the sink. The dishes of the dinner were still left, so I thought of washing them quietly, as I'd no other work now except for talking to Neera.

The cold wind blew in from outside, filling the room with coldness and defying the fact that it was summer. The air smelled of freedom for me to be exact. I didn't know why it was strange, maybe because I was doing the dishes at night when I was usually in my bed and it was all quiet and I would get up for a glass of water. When I thought of it, it totally contradicted my feelings. I could hear freedom from the wind that came in and caressed my locks and teased my body. But I couldn't understand it. It was sweet, but I couldn't tell from where the sweetness came. I gazed outside at the crescent in the sky, sighing upon the earth its pale moonlight that filtered through the leaves. I could hear crickets singing. Did insects gaze at the moon too? How did they feel about it? What was freedom for them?

The serenity was tasteful, like a spoon fed dish and yet I couldn't truly decode it. Deep in my thoughts, I didn't even noticed I'd washed all the dishes, and so, after having a glass of water and closing the kitchen window, I retreated back to my bed. Ava and Tarini were still sleeping, without paying attention to the on-goings happening in the house. My room was cold too, but this coldness was exciting, sending shivers down my spine and reminding me of Hatsune Miku's song 'Miku'.

'I'm on top of the world, because of you,' I hummed to myself after opening my laptop and going to BunnyGram. 'I do nothing that they could never do.'

Well, I actually do things others can't possibly do. Like daydream even while studying. Is it rare or common? Well, I don't care...

I talked to Neera freely over BunnyGram because I knew talking over phone was too risky. Not that we discussed something vulgar or inappropriate, but there were some 'school gossips' which I definitely didn't want my mother to see. She didn't know I'd a BunnyGram account in my laptop, and the guilt of hiding something sometimes came over me. And then there were some more things which were worth hiding due to privacy, so that guilt took off.

The question that teased me was, did I even need privacy? After all, whatever I was doing was still out of her sight, so it was wrong...

N: Where were you? Busy?

T: No, I'd to do the dishes. The two potatoes are sleeping on the couch tonight.

...

N: Hey, can I call you?

T: Sure? Is something wrong?

N: Everything's fine. I just wanted to talk to you. Over phone. Like hear your actual voice.

I smiled to myself and silenced my phone so that the ringtone doesn't wake them up. Neera's name flashed over my screen in matter of seconds and I picked it up.

'Hey, I hope I'm not disturbing you, am I?' Neera said in an exhausted voice.

'No you didn't, you never do.'

I shut down the laptop, switched off the desk light and lied down on my bed, looking at the bioluminescent starry stickers on the ceiling. The moon was in the middle, slightly away from the fan, and the creativity had been done when it used to be Tarini's room.

'Is something wrong?' I asked her again.

'No, it's just... I feel worthless sometimes,' Neera said, but her voice cracked a little. She took a deep breath and continued. 'It's not like I'm victimizing myself but I feel useless on this land sometimes.'

'You aren't useless,' I said, but she seemed to be spilling out her emotions which had been bottled for too long, so I let her continue, saying I was there to listen everything.

'It feels like nobody actually cares here at my house, and that, there's a gender difference. I know I have all the pleasures a teenager imagines at this age but they feel hollow. Maybe because I don't want such pleasures but to lead a normal life like anybody else. It's suffocating sometimes. It's like drowning in the ocean but with bliss. Like you're drowning which is fatal but it's bliss, so it makes the drowning look better than life.'

'Tell me what happened.'

'Some guests came today,' she started. 'The man was my father's best friend, his close member who accompanies him in his party meetings. He even brought his wife and their son, who is the same age as we are. As usual you know, I had to help mummy bring the snacks and the cold drinks to the living room table. But as I followed her, my brother came from the other room looking at his mobile phone and collided with me. The drinks fell on the lady's saree and she was drenched from the chest. Even the glasses broke. And do you know who got the scolding? Me... It's always me, be it a mistake done by my brother or some other male of the house, it's always me. I was having a panic attack and amidst that, my mother made me stand in front of the guests and scolded me. The man literally had to get up to separate my mother from me and I ran away to my room. I just... hate it here. I wish they were more fair and logical. I... don't know how I should feel...'

I could hear her sniff through the phone and wondered what I should say to comfort her. Saying something negative would eventually lead her to hate her family, which she already did. So I tried to console her, like I always did.

'I understand,' I said. 'Don't cry Neera. It hurts me here when you cry. You empower me all the time and if you're only going to break down, what will happen to me?'

'I know,' she said in a withering voice. It was all quiet in her area, so maybe she was in her room. 'I just wanted to open it out to you. I know they aren't going to change. I wish they were just kinder and fairer.'

'Hey now, don't be sad,' I said cheerfully. I was really bad at making people happy. 'Everything will be fine soon. At least, your father loves you more than anyone else. And, you remember our mantra don't you? The one we thought would suit us, in class ninth?'

'Yeah I do.'

'So say it together with me.'

I took a deep breath and we both began.

'So I'll say hello, again hello
What is there to be done?
Find a mechanist, a mechanism
Working one by one.
With a busted up database,
I'm losing the chase,
BUT I'll say hello, again hello
And turn to face the sun!'

I heard her giggle on the other side as she sang with me. This was the song which bound us together in hard times, when we needed to get up from the darkness. I sang it often, and we'd divided parts of who'll sing which part. I sang the last part in a low voice and she listened.

'Hello! How are you?
Hello! What can I do?
Hello! How are you?
Hello! What can I do?'

'Hello AI Tara, I'm feeling good,' Neera answered and we giggled. I heard for any noise in the living room for a moment and got back to talking. 'Now what you can do is listen to me. I found something interesting the other day and I'll tell you that.'

'Okay.'

'So there's this idiom we've heard, "To the moon and back". I found its deeper meaning the other day on Nailterest, which explained that it means the vastness of affection one has for their loved one.'

'It's like a hyperbole,' I said.

'Yeah, and there's a scientific meaning as well. Every day, our heart creates enough energy to drive a truck twenty miles and in a lifetime, it is equivalent to driving to the moon and back. Isn't it meaningful? To love someone for your lifetime with all the blood your heart pumps.'

'Uh huh.'

'I found this so interesting, I decided to make a special page about this in my journal, but you know it depends on the mood. Nonetheless, I'll bring my journal and some printouts so that we can work on it together.'

'Uh huh.'

'Are you sleeping? Well it's already late and we're meeting tomorrow at your house. So have a good night's sleep!'

'And don't think about it too much. Remember that you aren't useless, especially not to me.'

'Hehe, thanks! Good night bunny. Bye.'

'Bye.'

The call ended but I was still thinking about what she'd found out. I knew it already and I even knew who deserved to listen it from my mouth.

For Neera. To the moon and back.

I found myself lying on my back on a cool but hard platform, looking directly up at the sky; wait, it wasn't the sky, because the reflections that came down on me were cool, and it reminded me of the pictures under the ocean waters. It *was* the ocean. And I was *under* it.

I found my coordination perfectly normal, like any human has on land and I could even breathe without any difficulty or grasp for breath. I lifted myself up and looked at my surroundings. There were circus tents everywhere, like the ones that used to be set up in earlier times. They looked clean and new and I could even hear a faint song playing from inside of them.

I remember that song. Hello, again.

It was faint yet it made me happy for some reason. I knew I was in a dream but I could control it. Above me, I saw colourful fishes swimming gracefully along with rabbits. Rabbits?

'Weird,' I mumbled, looking at them as one of them swam towards me and others followed the white fur ball. I reached for it slowly and it even let me pet its white head.

'This is so cool!' I exclaimed with uncontrollable joy, looking at the colours and the environment. I walked forward hearing the faint tunes hit me as I hummed to them, and soon enough, I was out of the circus with the song still carrying to me like it was following me too. But the scene I saw in front of myself was too great to celebrate.

A huge road lay horizontally in front of me, and it was like any other road, but did any normal road have *eighteen* lanes? I definitely hadn't seen that. The way to the other footpath, as my eyes could see through the cars and buses travelling across like bugs, was too far away and I assumed it would take ages for someone to get to the other side if they weren't that great in dodging the incoming traffic. I blinked at my bunny partners, who were now sitting on my head and shoulders, looking at each other. There was a roundabout painted in horizontal yellow and black strips at a distance which had a radius about the size of fountain, but instead of a fountain in between, it had a huge banyan tree underneath which was a small temple of Lord Shiva, as I spotted from the black stone. At the other end, adjoining to the pathway was a petrol pump and beside that, another way separating the famous jewellery stores and other huge buildings. Trees were lined neatly on the other side and it somewhat represented the picture of a familiar place which I couldn't identify at that moment.

'So, I've to cross this?' I asked, but of course, no reply came. But that was what happened in such dreams didn't it?

What if I find something cool on the other side?

And just as I was thinking, I saw a wave of tsunami spawn from thin air, and wash over the pathway. To my surprise, none of the buses or cars were washed away, as if an invisible shield was protecting them. In the wave came out several colours which could be seen if one held a pearl in the sunshine and the scenery was mesmerizing. I breathed in the fantasy events that were happening with me, and soon the waves lowered and what I saw was something I'd always wished to happen to me in reality.

An ultramarine scaled blue dragoness was sitting neatly on her haunches, looking at me with her brilliant copper golden eyes. Her under scales were the same colour as her eyes, reflecting the sunlight around her and almost forming a halo of rainbow. She was bigger than the cars but slightly shorter than the height of buses with her blue wings patterned with golden triangles folded neatly behind her. She didn't say anything. But I'd a lot to say.

'Ambience!' I gasped, looking at her with my eyes wide in awe. I knew her name. I knew every single detail about her. Because I'd made her myself. My first ever dragoness which I'd penned down and even drawn once which didn't come out well but her description definitely did. Ambience lowered her long neck and gazed at me, allowing me to see her copper spikes. I peered at her and realized her scales weren't fully ultramarine, but reduced to waves of lighter shades of blue as they ascended to her underbelly from her spikes. Her long tail thick at the end was fading in lighter colours as well. The patterns were hard to look at though.

'Wow! How do I reach you?' I put my hands on my hips and looked at the traffic. It was unusual, and the buses and cars were speeding, literally. No way was I going to make it to the other side without getting squashed under one of the vehicles. I waved at Ambience, hoping she would fly to me, but she lied on her forearms and looked at me, as if urging *me* to come to her instead.

'You aren't going to come to your creator?' I shrieked uselessly, because in all the speeding sounds she wasn't going to hear my blabber. Saying that sounded awkward, but that was what occurred to me. 'What do you want me to do?'

Ambience did nothing and just watched. I sighed and looked on both the sides of the first lane. The vehicles were going from right to left. I began calculating when the time would be enough to pass through them. But there was a problem which stopped me from jumping to my death instantly. Even if I jumped, there was no space for me to land safely and plan my next move. My swiftness was going to be one-timer and this was the worst because I really wanted to meet Ambience as if it was something that mattered in my life.

I looked at the first lane and then at the second. For some seconds, I could make out a gap between three lanes, and then so on it went. An impatient me jumped and dodged the near attack from the vehicles but as soon as I jumped to the third lane, a car hit me and before I could feel anything or even see what death looked like, I woke up breathing heavily and my heart drumming inside my chest. I could hear it clearly in the silent and cold room.

'What the actual heck?' I said breathlessly and waited for everything to settle inside me. It was one of those dreams where you are just walking down the stairs and then you slip out of nowhere and wake up gasping for breath like a fish out of water. I frowned at Ambience's drawing stuck on the wall where my study table was and got out of the bed. It was still eight in the morning, and I'd received a message in my mobile phone. From Neera.

N: Hey bunny. I'll be coming at around eleven today. We've a lot of things to do!

The message was posted at around seven. I texted her back.

T: Sure.

After cleaning my bed, I came out to the living room where my sisters were busy having breakfast all alone. I looked at them for a second; Tarini was busy talking to someone over the phone which was pinned on her shoulder with her tilted head while Ava was scrolling on her phone as well. I sighed but they didn't notice it so I proceeded towards the bathroom and freshened myself up.

'I've prepared garlic bread for breakfast, so eat it up and wash your plate,' Tarini instructed me while sliding her feet in her leather sandals. She flung her bag over her shoulder and hurried outside the house, where Sania was waiting for her on her scooty. The two of them waved me goodbye and rushed away. Even Ava left soon. I knew they were going to be back by five, but even those hours made me feel like I owned the house. I feasted on the breakfast, which contained a big slice of cheese on each of the three slices of bread. Tarini always made it a different way, and all of us liked her cooking too. Ava on the other hand, was just like me; the two of us only knew how to cook instant noodles and considered ourselves master chefs if the gravy was thick and juicy.

I put on my favourite science show, which was telecasted every day at around ten in the morning and went on till half past ten. I wasn't allowed to watch TV but since I'd a little freedom, there was no harm in doing so. I wasn't doing it for fun but for knowledge.

'And whenever you've to skate, make sure to aid yourself properly!' Maniesh Paul announced in a funny accent which made me giggle.

Soon, it was time for Neera to come, and for some reason, she exactly rang the doorbell at eleven. I couldn't be much more accurate myself.

'Hi!' she greeted me excitedly. I saw she was wearing a dark maroon pleated skirt which went down her knees, and a white coloured small top covered with a small cotton half-sleeved jacket black in colour. She closed her floral umbrella and put it on the shoe rack before entering and I locked the door, peering from the window for any strangers.

'It's really hot outside, but what a relief here!' Neera breathed, smiling at me.

'Because I forgot to turn the AC off in the morning, so much of the cold air stayed in,' I explained to her. 'Why do you have your hair down if you feel hot? Should I tie it?'

'No, it's fine,' she grinned, sitting on the couch and throwing her sling bag on one side. 'I don't want to take away your signature hairstyle.'

I smiled at her. No matter what season it was, I always kept my hair in a neat bun, be it oily or dry (dry bun was a pain in the back with small hairs coming out like antennas), be it summer or winter, be it a party or a meet-up with the girls. It'd really become my signature style and each of my friend in our group knew well about it.

'I'll go grab some cold drink for you,' I told her to escape her flirty gaze and slipped into the kitchen. A bottle of Thumbs Up was kept in, unopened. Our mother had forbidden us to drink cold drinks, saying they were bad and over time, I too had developed a habit of avoiding them. But I couldn't imply the same thing to others easily. Neera too never drank carbonated drinks usually, but if the bottle had been kept for the guests, why not give it to her too? She was a guest of the house after all. And to my surprise, even my mother had instructed me to serve Neera with the drink if she ever visited the house in her absence.

'And don't drink it yourself!' she'd snapped.

Well, I'll just get some cold water from the pot.

'Thanks,' Neera said, taking the glass from me while I sat on the couch adjacent to her. She sipped at it and kept it on the table, reaching out for her bag to fish out something. Her bag caught my eye. On the brown sandy colour was a camel weaved with colourful woollen threads and mirrors decorating the camel's neck. I wondered where she even got these from.

'See, I brought our journal back and I've written a lot of things,' she bubbled with excitement. I took the book from her and looked at it while she tied her hair into a ponytail with a rubber band. The cover was adorned with one more sticker of an eye, apart from all the rainbow stickers of Neera. With a black background the letters 'TARA AND NEERA'S SECRETS' flashed brightly and gave pleasure to ones' eyes. We'd written many things about school, home and friends in the journal we were sharing together; all the incidents that happened while the teacher was busy writing something on the board, how the class was teamed up even if someone got scolded (after they were done laughing), how the girl gang spent time during the PE period (it was always free because the sports teacher was satisfied with the athlete girl only), how Neera and I did pranks on each other (it was Neera for most of the time who made the boys think she was in relation with a boy to avoid her stalkers).

'About last night, I wrote not much because I already told you what happened,' Neera said. I saw some glittering unicorn stickers in her hands and even coloured gel pens to decorate the page. 'So today, we'll decorate a page on the theme of moon. What do you say?'

'Sounds fun,' I grinned. She placed her rainbow set on the coffee table and after taking another sip from our cold drinks (mine was the cold water), we began doing our work. Neera took one corner and began making galaxy using her brush pens and the white pen, while in the middle of the page, I drew a rough but almost perfect circle for the moon. As a good feature, the pages of the journal were thick and the colours didn't soak on the back side that much, which enabled much of our creativity to be shown.

Neera finished the background while I finished the moon, which wasn't that good as compared to her art style, but I still found it surprised as to how I was still good at art. Maybe it was because of the term grades we got for finishing off an art project, which in turn boosted my art style and made it hard to forget. My mother didn't let me do it. She thought it was just a waste of time.

'You know I got a message from Swastik the other day,' Neera said, looking at me as we leaned back on the couch to get some rest.

'Wow! That boy never stops his tricks does he?' I frowned. 'What did he say though?'

'Nothing, just random talks,' she rolled her eyes and smirked. 'But as you'd told me about him, he acted just like it! Sweet talks to woo me. But nothing's going to work.'

'He tried because you're pretty and you're even closer to me,' I said. If it'd been any casual talk, I wouldn't have been able to say it to her. 'It'd be better if you just block him. I don't care what he says anymore. He's just a dumb rock thinking he's smart enough to manipulate everyone.'

'Yeah right,' Neera nodded. 'And as if you aren't pretty.'

'Not more than you.'

'Idiot.'

'Anyways, just listen to what he said next to me,' Neera said, grinning. I didn't know if it was my imagination, or her cheeks had actually become red. 'Then, he began talking randomly about how good I was and how I helped everyone around me and all. Even I began to think like, boy when did I do this? I mean, I do help people but not those who think I'm some servant.'

'He used to say the same things to me too,' I smiled at her. 'What a big jerk!'

'And listen,' she continued. 'I wasn't even in the mood to talk to him, and this idiot was constantly messaging me even when I didn't reply to him. Like how far can you drop your self-respect? Huh! And upon everything, he messaged right at the time when I'd to call you! I don't like it when somebody interrupts my conversation with you. So I said this. "Please don't disturb me now. My boyfriend won't like it".'

The both of us began laughing loudly. I liked it when Neera tried to understand why I wasn't talking to one particular person and then avoid them to keep the fact alive that my best friend was not someone else. She and I shared the same mind and nobody could tear us apart. I especially hated Swastik because of how he acted all mysterious and played tricks on innocent girls attracted by his handsome face (I was attracted only because of his behaviour for some reason). Neera knew it and so she always stayed away from it, but her beautiful face attracted him like a dog to her. At first, I thought it was not good to interrupt with Neera's social circle and how she acted with everyone because it was her personal choice, but then it was her who told me that a best friend was supposed to support her best friend in good decisions. Personal choice didn't matter in this. It was for the knowledge of both of us to stay away from such boys.

'Now he'll be out there trying to find out who my boyfriend is,' Neera wiped a tear from her eye, still giggling. 'I wonder how he'll do that. Find my invisible boyfriend.'

'He's a real idiot,' I said. 'I just hate him with all my heart and all the energy it takes to hate someone. I can't believe I fell for a boy like him! Yuck!'

'It's fine, we need experience with such boys to avoid getting trapped by them later in life,' Neera said. 'I know it was too early for such things, but now, we're matured enough to understand the difference between right and wrong. I'll say, it was quite important.'

'Right enough.'

'Hey, it's almost one now. Didn't the girls say they'll call at one?'

'Oh yeah.'

'Let's check the group.'

The group chat was already on. The girl gang, which consisted of five of us, was discussing who should start the call. Prasanna said she would, and soon enough, we were face timing our friends.

'Aye! The both of you are together?' Anya exclaimed, and the other nodded in surprise too. I almost lost control and hid my face with a wide grin while Neera smiled at them.

'I was just visiting her house you know,' she replied to them. 'Just doing random stuff.'

I reached out to pick the empty glasses but Neera just pulled me to her and held my waist so I stay stuck to her. I couldn't understand what happened for a moment and I could only feel her heat. Everybody was clearly looking at me, and I even saw Prasanna's smug face as if she'd unlocked an achievement.

'Okay now, so first let's decide the time,' Anya continued as if she didn't saw what happened. I could barely focus on her words without getting distracted by Neera's random movements. She had her hand up on her shoulder now, keeping me in place to avoid losing me.

'Is everyone comfortable at five in the evening?' Nayani asked.

'No, four is good for me, because mummy won't let me stay out for too long,' Prasanna disagreed. 'And we shouldn't stay late outside as well.'

'Four's good for me too,' Anya nodded her head.

'Same for us,' Neera said.

'Now, where shall we meet?'

'Outside the parking lot.'

'Is anyone going to bring their parents or any adult?'

Neera looked at me and I realized all the other girls were looking at me too. They knew that one problem was with me. I knew Ava and Tarini wouldn't come with me. And if I told mummy about our plan, she was going to blast with anxiety in Pune's hotel. Or the house at which she was staying.

'I need to ask my mother about that,' I told them. 'My sisters would be at college so there's no one to accompany. I wonder if she'd let me go alone with you guys.'

'It's fine, we'll ask her right now after the call,' Neera said, smiling at me. Her face was so close, I'd to look down to avoid making strange faces. I nodded.

After some more boring discussions about dress code and money, the meeting ended. It was almost half past one, and Neera quickly packed her stuff in her camel bag. She surprisingly held my hand and looked deep into my eyes. I was pretty sure she could see the redness flash on my cheeks.

'I'll stay until you talk to her,' she said warmly. I was touched by her gesture, but thinking about my mother's words made my stomach lurch. I knew what she was going to say. I knew it was never going to be yes.

'No it's okay, I'll talk to her,' I said in a half-smile. 'I hope she says yes. I'll inform you tonight about it.'

'Okay, but don't be late.'

'Yeah.'

I walked to her outside till the gate and after waving me goodbye, she parted, opening her umbrella in the summer heat. I would've asked her to stay, had Tarini and Ava prepared something to eat but they were going to need some time to adjust to the hard-work. So all I'd was instant noodles, which I cooked while watching some cartoons and afterwards, went for a quick nap. For some time, I couldn't sleep because I kept thinking of some ways which would sound less harmful to mom. For her, going out with friends was one of the thousand ways of wasting time for someone like me, because it was not 'knowledgeable'. For her, a valedictorian wasn't supposed to do these things. It was a literal harm to my studies for her. At some points she was right, but not for all. Thinking about all these made me sleepy and at last, I dozed off into a dreamless nap.

'Hi mom, what are you doing?'

'Nothing dear, just taking some breeze in the village air. I wish I could bring you too but you've to study. Plus, Tarini and Ava can't be trusted completely with household. They'll make my house a mess!'

'Ha! That's so true! The last night, I'd to wash the dishes after completing my studies. The two couch potatoes slept on the sofa while eating popcorn and watching TV.'

'What? They're really a mess! I'll take their class after I come back. What did you have for breakfast and lunch?'

'Tarini made garlic bread for breakfast but she didn't have time to prepare the lunch. It takes time to adjust and take care like you mummy. I'll try to her help her with it.'

'Yeah right, dear. But try to avoid cheesy and oily food. They're not good for your health. You won't want to get sick, would you? Anyways, anything else?'

'Neera came over today so I served her the cold drink we keep for guests.'

'Oh sweet. That girl's the only one whom you can actually trust. Her birthday's this month isn't it?'

'Yes, but don't worry about it. I've something in my mind. I'll give her the best gift.'

'Right, and what's that going to be?'

'Something made by myself. Because before the vacations, she made a bracelet for me with my favourite charm.'

'That's good.'

I heard someone calling her from behind. Probably my father.

'Alright, anything else you want to say?'

I hesitated for a moment. I didn't want this sweetness to end. But I'd to tell her before the night dropped down. So taking a deep breath, I said it.

'Mummy, the girls are planning to visit the mall tomorrow. Neera is coming too, so can I join them? I promise I would be back by six and I'll call you frequently to tell you about my on-goings.'

Silence. Those three moments felt heavier than the science books. I felt as if I was sitting in front of the panel of judges for UPSC interview.

'When are you going? At what time?'

'We've decided four o' clock in the evening. And we won't stay out for too long. Just window shop and come back. We won't even go out to eat anything. Just come back home.'

Another seconds passing in silence.

Please let me go.

'But you know you can't take Ava and Tarini with you. They'll be in the college till late, and I don't want to leave you alone. I know Neera is a good girl, but going out in the evening for "window shopping" sounds worthless and a waste of time, you know.'

I didn't say anything.

'And your coaching classes are starting from tomorrow. You won't want to miss out the first day would you? And you need to get more serious with your studies. You have boards dear.'

Thank you very much for reminding me the horrors of not listening to you.

'Plus, you know the competition. And those girls don't care about studying. Tell me if I'm wrong.'

'No you're right in that. But that doesn't influence me.'

'You may not understand it now Tara, but you do get influenced. Parents understand it, not children.'

Now that was the trigger point for me. As if I was a trash who knew nothing what happened to me. I hated this line. I hated it.

'Go if you want.'

That last line almost came out in an instruction. Not even the half-hearted reply mothers gave to their naughty children and the children took it as yes. I couldn't do it. I'd been coded not to.

OBEY

Before I could answer, she hung up and I was left staring at the notes on the wall in front of me. My lips were parted for a fraction of seconds but then closed as I put my phone down with full force on the Physics book. But upon giving it a second thought, she was actually right. I didn't have to buy anything and moreover if I thought about, I realized my mother was completely right. How could I've not thought of it? How did I become so irresponsible? Wasn't I supposed to not disobey her so that I don't face problems?

Follow your mother and you'll be disciplined and well-mannered. You'll be the ideal child and the ideal student. You shouldn't waste your time Tara. Anything that's not studying is a waste of time. Only my knowledge can let me stay at the top of the mountain.

'Alright, I guess I'll apologise to her about it later,' I mumbled and messaged Neera that I wasn't going to come. Putting my mobile on silent mode, I began solving the numericals in the silence of the evening.

3

'You're coming to my birthday aren't you?' Neera asked me as we walked into the school canteen. I didn't reply. I knew I was going to, but I felt disconnected at the moment. I just wanted school to end. There was more comfort in between the poetry lines and sometimes, the Chemistry volumes.

'You're starting to doubt me too, huh?' I gave her a smirk but Neera didn't smile. She just looked at me while I sat beside her and opened the tiffin. 'You know I'll surely come.'

'No, because I thought your mom won't let you to, so I was planning to bring my cake to a restaurant near your house,' she said as a matter-of-fact. For Neera, most of the things I imagined and thought were awkward were actually possible. Like she could travel anywhere around the city because her father had appointed personal drivers for his children. Of course her mother was wrathful but her father wasn't.

'No it's fine, mom thinks you're a good girl,' I replied. I found her tone irritating in this matter. It was as if she was doing me a favour. But I didn't show it. 'She'll allow me to go.'

'Good.'

I ate a spoonful of poha which mom had made for me and it lighted my taste buds. Neera's tiffin had sandwiches but she just poked the crisped bread for some seconds and finally lifted it to her mouth. Since the school had reopened after two weeks, she hadn't been talking like before, and it was always me now who started the conversation.

'Is something wrong?' I asked her. She didn't nod nor said anything and I waited for her response.

Must be that dumbo Swastik.

'Why are you making a face similar to a shrimp?' I said with the most serious face but she didn't laugh and I'd to take out my handkerchief to hide my smile. Even if it wasn't funny to my friends, I found my dumb jokes funny.

'Nothing,' Neera said and ate quietly. I waited for some time yet again and then poked her again on the shoulder, like I always did to annoy her.

'Come on now, tell me,' I snapped. Maybe she was angry with me. But for what? I hadn't done anything. Or had I? 'Being silent won't get you what you want. What is pestering you?'

'I'm just thinking about the project and the exams,' she breathed out. 'What they gave us is so big, it's going to take a lot of time. How will we even manage to study?'

'Oh so that's what it is,' I laughed. 'That's not even a problem dummy. We're going to be in pairs. And you know who's going to be with you.'

She smiled finally and it relieved my heart.

'But it's not an ordinary project, do you know that?' she said. She was finally eating her sandwich without delving deeper in thoughts.

'What is it about?'

'Our Physics lecturer is going to tell us today.'

After the lunch break was over, we proceeded back to our class. The Physics lecturer entered the class and we greeted him. He was at least six feet tall or maybe taller than that, and he still had the build of a man in his thirties. Usually, Mr Anthony was always busy with his ATL projects and his and his team's hard work had brought them many certificates and prizes in the AI competitions at regional and national levels as well. If we showed interest in his projects while we visited the ATL lab, he was likely to explain each and every mechanism of it.

The white haired man looked at us for a second and then, putting down some of his files he sat on the table and asked me if everyone was back from the break. I took a quick look around the class and reported who was out. Just like a robot.

'Okay, I'll see them later,' Sir Anthony said and then looked at the class cheerfully. 'Today, we shall discuss about the science project. Let me check my file first.'

I could hear groans from the last benches; my bench was behind two benches in the third row, behind all the first benchers who were too keen to separate themselves out from the giggles and the jokes. Those were the ones who acted too prim and proper, as if they were the most disciplined. But after seeing the photographs they captured while being the toilet, using it as if it belonged to them all, I was happy with my place. Not that the last benchers were any good, they pretty much annoyed me with their stupid question to teachers for disrupting the class but it was much better to be with the original faces than with the two faced.

'Okay, here it is,' Sir Anthony drew attention towards him. I was about to get distracted by Neera's random shuffling and her resting her leg on the side of my leg but I stayed focused. 'Now be quiet. So you all must be knowing we've a science fair coming up as well.'

'Not the science fair too,' Neera groaned and looked at me.

'So like you all had made working models in standard ten and eleven, this year too we shall follow the same procedure. Make working models for projects. Marks will be granted to all if it's correctly shown and well-presented and the best ones will be put up in the fair next week. The selected project makers should make sure to keep their project safe till we take them for submission. As for the selection rounds, the projects will be checked on Friday, so you all better not give reasons of forgetfulness or something else. Be responsible and complete the assigned part.'

'Also, be sure to make a presentation about the project. It can include the theory, the scientist who made that theory, the working *shown* and not written in points, and other things to make it interesting. And make the project according to your level and concepts. Don't bring an air conditioner to me.'

'Sir, is it an individual project?' one of the boys sitting behind us asked, raising his hand.

'Oh right, I forgot to mention that it's a group project,' Sir Anthony exclaimed. 'You can make groups of two, three or four. Not more than four and not less than two. Make it clear and choose your leader wisely. The teammates should corporate and help the leader. Don't whine about the members. You're responsible to choose them. Now you can discuss if you want. I've some work to complete.'

He sat down and began scribbling something in the diary he'd brought. Neera slouched down on her folded hands and hid her face between them. I fiddled with my pen while looking around when she poked me.

'What are we going to make?' she asked, already giving the look of a lazy girl.

'I'll need to search up some good projects,' I said. 'Don't you want ours to get selected?'

'I do,' she nodded. 'The last time, it was just a normal biology model, but let's think something out of the box and try to win this time.'

'Sure.'

'I think I'll come over and work with you,' she smiled. 'I can even stay for the night, because we only have four days left now. Why do they always have to give us projects in the middle of the year when we have exams on our heads and that too when the deadline is around four days after?'

'That's the tale of most of the schools,' I smiled back. 'Anyways, will your parents allow you to stay at my house for the night?'

'Of course they would. Mother doesn't care much about me being with you and father doesn't poke his nose in matters of studies. I'll be good.'

'Okay, make sure to bring your stuff then. I'll send you the list of things you need to buy today afternoon. And on which day will you come over?'

'See, we don't have school on Wednesday and Thursday, so I'll stay for the whole day on Wednesday and we'll try to complete most of the model work on that day. I'm not good at making presentations so you'll handle it. Leave the model to me. Just tell me what is to be done and I'll have it ready.'

'Thank god I have you,' I grinned. 'It takes me time to prepare a good presentation. It'd have been hard without an artist by my side.'

'Don't mention it.'

After the school was over, I kept thinking about the project as I walked down the street under the merciless rays of the sun. With May coming to an end, it was becoming much hotter and I wondered if Monsoon will come or not. Tarini and Ava were in the college as usual and mom had said she wouldn't be able to pick me up due to work so I'd to walk alone. Worse part, I'd forgot to carry an umbrella. With each passing minute, the picture of my fair skin being tanned flashed in between the concepts of Physics and Chemistry.

What could I possibly make to impress the teachers and the judges?

Wiping my face every minute with my handkerchief, I walked past some open stores with shopkeepers lazing on their chairs in front of table fans. Checking my pockets for money, I found a twenty rupee note.

I can get a chocolate ice cream bar.

A nearby shop had a deep freezer placed beside the glass door and as I looked up at the name, I found out it was a bakery. The owner looked like a man of sixties. Without further thinking, I bought a chocolate bar and continued the painful journey to my home. The coldness along with the heat provided a weird relief in the breeze-less afternoon, with crickets singing in the bushes and stray dogs resting under the parked cars of people. Usually, mummy would never leave me on my own to come back from school, but it was something really urgent in her school and she'd left her message describing me that.

Mummy: I've to prepare the report cards of the students so it'd probably take me longer. Don't wait for me and have your lunch. I'll buy something from outside to eat.

Being the class teacher of sixth standard, her job asked her more than her appointed salary sometimes, and so to help her out, I'd often make her something good to snack on once she was home in the evening. She appreciated my skills but I got scolded for not studying as well. That scolding had sweetness in it sometimes.

As I walked in the quietness of the street, I saw a cardboard box kept outside a shop shutter which was closed. At first, I ignored it because it wasn't any marble statue to look at, but it began moving. I stopped to confirm the movement because I was sure it'd been an illusion. But the box moved again and this time, with a greater force as if the thing inside it was trying to get out. The flaps were loosely shut and almost open. Picturing a small puppy in the box or a small cat (Or a rat if I imagined it too far), I moved to the box after finishing my bar quickly to see what was inside. I was not planning to get scratched if it was a cat, but my curiosity wasn't going to let me back off or sleep in the night without checking what was inside. The box began moving frantically until I took a look around the empty street. Then, I pinned it with power to the ground and opened the flaps.

Inside was a white fur ball with huge bead-like shiny black eyes embedded on it like obsidian and long ears that stood straight at the sight of me looking at it. For a moment, both of us maintained that gaze and then, the bunny broke it by jumping out of the box and into my arms which caught it with reflex. I gasped and almost dropped it but since it wasn't struggling nor biting me, I took it calmly and petted its smooth white fur. For a colour like it and a fur like it, the bunny almost felt like a being from another planet that was trying to mimic the animals of the earth and probably eat me another second by growing tentacles and sharp canines. But the look it gave me warmed my heart.

'How can someone leave you out here?' I asked as if pacifying a child, while stroking its ears gently. 'It's weird for someone to leave you with such care in a cardboard box. But at least, they'd some humanity left in them.'

The bunny made a strange squeaking sound, and I, who had zero experience with bunnies, thought it was happy. Well, it sure did look like it was glad. Its fur was somewhat warmer, maybe because of the rays that managed to penetrate upon it. I feared if it was sick or something, but it looked completely healthy. While holding it, I took another peak in the box and saw a paper folded in it. Carefully picking it up, I opened it and read. The writing was the most beautiful I'd ever seen, but it set an image in my mind that the owner was pretty much planning to leave the bunny outside to be taken by someone else, or to get devoured by the stray dogs and cats either way.

If someone is reading this, then I'd be obliged if you take Snow with you and take care of him. You'll have the blessings with you.

'That was pretty short,' I narrowed my eyes and stuffed it in my pocket. The last line did seem weird and I could make out nothing of it. I glanced at Snow and then at the emptiness around. And then at Snow again.

'Now what shall I do about you?' I asked, lifting him up to my face. He tilted his head and blinked at me in the cuteness which made me squeak happily. But then flashed my mother's image in my mind. She was not going to tolerate me bringing a rabbit home. And that too when we'd an aquarium with two turtles of two different species.

Those two were enough to let us experience the difficulty one had in keeping pets. And bringing a rabbit home was surely going to take away my freedom, since mom would think I actually bought it from the pet shop. But on the other hand, I couldn't leave him alone here. I had a plan though.

The report card for the first term was to be shown in the first week of July. I was confident that I was going to get above ninety five percent this time (Last time, it was ninety two but it disappointed my mother), and claiming the title of valedictorian yet again was not a topic of doubt at all. My plan was to reveal Snow after I got the report card, and narrate the story of how I'd found him on the road, exaggerating that I'd to protect it from the dogs. Then, mom would not have any chance but to let me have him as a pet, since I fulfilled her wish. It was only the allowance that was necessary. Otherwise, it was going to be mom herself who would take care of him afterwards.

But the PT meeting is after a month, if I remember. Where will I keep him for such a long time? Probably hide him. But what will I feed him? Won't mom get suspicious if she found vegetable shreds into my room? I'd be so dead.

Looking at Snow's huge eyes, I decided to take it as a mission and carried him home while covering him with my shadow.

Soon enough, I was at the main gate and trying to look inside through the small gap in between the curtains of the windows, I opened the gate and entered like a thief. According to my watch, there should've been no one at home. Taking out the spare keys, I unlocked the door and closed it after entering. Keeping Snow on the white marbled floor, I stroked him again and looked at the turtles in the aquarium. Both of them were sitting on the stony ground, looking at me with their round burly eyes. They glanced at the bunny with great interest, which made me wonder if animals could talk to each other even if they were of different kind.

'Stay here while I prepare your bed,' I told Snow and he seemed to understand what I was saying. So leaving him there, I went in. I couldn't bring him to the bed yet because I'd some paperwork scattered on the bed and desk. And I definitely didn't want Snow to eat them.

I'd a makeshift bed kept under my bed which was earlier occupied by the two turtles when they were less than three months old. It was a small cardboard box painted vibrantly like a house from outside, and it even had the interior of the house in the inner side. Most of it was just plain drawing to make the box bright and for comfort, I'd placed a soft pastel pink fur that had initially been my old sling bag's cover. It acted as a comfy sleeping place. I fetched Snow from the living room and placed him neatly in the box.

'Stay here and don't hop away somewhere,' I told him, wagging my index finger at him. 'Otherwise, both of us will be homeless.'

He wheezed, as if agreeing. I put him near my bed in the open and changed my clothes.

'Don't look at me,' I snarled and as if he understood it properly, he put his little white paws on his eyes. I thought I would die of cuteness right there. While freshening myself, I wondered if he would eat carrots, as people said about rabbits, so fishing out a carrot, some leaves of a fresh cabbage Ava had bought the previous night to make noodles, and a slice of apple from my own share to feed him. I served Snow in a plate and he began feasting on them hungrily, gnawing the veggies like a machine.

'Now I just need to hide you for some weeks,' I told him. *Some* weeks.

As I'd promised Neera to send her the list of things for the project, I got to work. I was planning to make a smart waste recycling machine which would sort waste in their respective categories.

Just a little research on it.

There were several videos on how to make one. The last time in standard ten, I'd tried to make a Tesla coil initially but it'd been a bad decision since it required a long length of copper wire to be wrapped around the pipe. And copper wire was quite expensive for my budget since nobody in my team was ready to contribute for it. So two days before the submission, I made a working model of heart with much effort and stressing my hands in the process. It didn't achieve many appreciations but many parents sure liked my way of explaining. Not to mention I was changing my lingual skills in between.

I prepared the list of items and emailed them to Neera. Meanwhile, I was keeping my eyes on Snow as he pawed at the soft fur and cuddled in it like a white snowball which was impossible to be spotted in the state I lived. He kept me hypnotized for some time with his activities and I began to fear, thinking I'd get distracted by his cute behaviour. But then when I remembered the time I'd bought the turtles, there'd been no distraction.

But rabbits are your favourite aren't they?

I shook my head violently and kept working for the project. Soon, it was four in the evening when I heard a knock on the door. I was sure it was my mother so I quickly hid Snow's box underneath my bed and hopped to the door to open it. My heart was racing inside my body. But I tried my best not to show it. I opened the door for my tired mother, who passed me an exhausted smile as she sat on the couch and leaned back, closing her eyes. I took her bag and kept it on the desk in my parent's room.

'Get me some water,' my mother said and I nodded though she still had her eyes closed. Sometimes, when I wondered about my mother, her physical features always came first to my mind. Even in the age of thirty seven, she was fit and fine, with a glossy skin inherited by her three daughters and sharp brown eyes which pinned anyone if she was angry. In the aspects of a strict English teacher, she fit all the quality types. Determined, poised with regal grace, and on the top of that, mother of three daughters among which one had the responsibilities of future. Well, everyone had that.

I handed her a glass of water and kept glancing at the open door of my room. My mother handed the glass to me and I took it back.

'Were you studying?' she asked. Still making sure I wasn't slacking off.

'Yes mummy.'

'Any notices from the school? About the report card? Did your teacher give any hints?'

'Well, she did praise me for my consistency. And as usual, I've the first place.'

'That, you don't need to tell me,' she said. The coldness was back in her. 'That's like your job. What I expect from you is the percentage. And your rank in the *whole section*.'

'I know.'

'Good.'

After she went into her room and closed the door behind, I returned back into my room and peeked into Snow's box. My heart leapt into my mouth when I saw the empty box. Sudden rush of adrenaline almost made me drop the vase kept on the side table by the bed. I looked around hurriedly for him, underneath my desk, behind other objects which could hide a small creature like him. Nothing.

OH GOD! Where did he go? If mummy finds this out, I'll be dead as a door nail.

Frantically rushing out of my room and then halting suddenly at the sight of my mother who looked at me with suspicion as she rolled her long hair into a bun, I tried to keep my gaze on the floor and acted as if I'd lost an item and not a stray rabbit I'd brought from the streets.

'What's up with you?' Mother asked, as she proceeded towards the kitchen.

'N-Nothing, just looking my eraser which rolled here,' I said, trying to calm my heart but I'd become stiff like a log. She eyed me for some time and went into the kitchen.

'Just go back and study,' she commanded. Behind her back, I began looking around the room underneath the couch, the aquarium and some hidden spots for rats. I tip-toed quietly to my parent's room but found nothing.

Where did he go???

The pressure on me this creature had made was more than the pressure my mother created for achieving better percentage according to her, at the moment. I could only imagine Snow getting spotted by mother and then I'll have a good round of scolding and beatings. Finding nothing in the living room and other rooms, I returned back to my bedroom and searched it well too. But my heart almost stopped when I heard another knock on the door. And voices of my sisters.

'Must be your sisters,' mummy said from the kitchen and I heard the gushing of water in the sink and silence again. If, by chance, Snow came out in front of her...

'I'll open the door!' I jumped in front of her before she could come out. Seeing my face, she frowned and pushed me aside gently.

'It's fine, go study,' she said and walked towards the door. I watched her and just as she opened the lock, I saw Snow coming out from behind the aquarium and looking at me while sniffing the floor. I was doomed. I signalled him to come to me but he turned his back to me and looked at Tarini and Ava at the door. In split seconds, I lunged at him but hearing my hurried steps, the three people looked at me curiously. Fortunately, Snow stood behind the door which opened inwards, so it was a goofy sight for my mother and sisters.

'Are you dancing or something?' Tarini asked. I shook my head violently and stood up straight, eyes shifting from Snow to mother and sisters.

I hope they don't see him. I hope they don't see him. I hope they don't see him!

'What's wrong with you?' my mother snapped, letting Tarini and Ava inside as they looked at me with questioning eyes. 'Aren't you supposed to study?'

'I was just helping,' I blurted and she sighed. Then walked back to the kitchen.

'Close the door then. And go to your room.'

I closed the door but Snow was already gone from the spot. Looking around wildly and almost twisting my neck nerves in the process, I looked down under the things again. And saw him. Behind the legs of my mother.

SNOW!

I wanted to shout but I couldn't. I'd done a huge mistake of hiding him. I should've found a better spot. Tip-toing behind my mother quietly, I attempted to take him in my hands. The smell of soya sauce lingered in my nose, and

I could tell that Paneer Chilli was being prepared for the dinner. Not my favourite but with the behaviour of mine, it was going to be ruined for everyone.

As fast as a jet, I reached out for him but he hoped to the side and my hands touched my mother's slippers. I scrambled up to my fours and slowly looked up as my mother whirled around with the wooden spatula in her hand covered with the red soya sauce she'd just poured which added to the delicious aroma of the sorted onions. She looked down at me with complete surprise on her face and I jumped up to my legs. To give me a heart attack, Snow jumped right in front of me and titled his head while gnawing his teeth in a carrot piece I'd given him.

Mummy looked down at her feet and my heart beat paced so fast, I thought it'd rip my chest and scatter on the floor. But she said nothing and looked up at me again, with brows turned in frown.

'What are you trying to do Tara?' my mother retorted. 'Since the time I've entered this house, I've been watching you dancing around the house? Are you hiding something from me?'

'N-No mummy,' I stammered but I knew that's where I made the mistake. I couldn't understand why she didn't exclaim about a bunny eating a carrot at her feet, but more than that, I knew I was in trouble.

'What? You've to say something?' she snapped at me like an alligator. 'Or it is about your marks?'

'Nothing, I'll just go back into my room,' I mumbled and turned to leave, taking a secret glance at me feet as Snow followed me. My mother didn't say anything. Nothing about Snow.

What is even happening?

I returned to my room and closed the door behind as soon as Snow got in. Picking him up and keeping him on my lap, I looked at him for some time with great interest. I even stroked his fur once and kept my hand on it to feel his warm body. He was breathing like any other animal. Looking at his eyes, he seemed like a normal bunny. Why did my mother not react?

'How come she didn't see you?' I lifted him up in the air and peered at him. Was I dreaming? Was it all just a long dream playing like a series in my mind, showcasing my whole life to me like a masquerade and I'm going to wake up any second now to start this play again? On second thought, it felt like one of my stories becoming true. Where mythical creatures disguised themselves as normal animals and lived among us. I wondered if Snow was about to transform into a dragon.

'Tell me, can you speak?' I asked, putting him on the desk in front of him and almost whispering. 'Can you talk like us? Or are you some shape-shifter? Do you have some quest?'

'You talk a lot!' Snow suddenly said in a voice of a young boy, sweet and small yet powerful enough to make me gasp loudly. My hands involuntarily moved over to my mouth and my gaze shifted to the closed door of my room. I was trying to hear if my mother had heard it, but she hadn't as I heard her talking to Ava. I looked back at Snow with eyes which were becoming wider than they actually were. His eyes looked annoyed if it wasn't my imagination, but as I stared at him, he jumped up and a platform formed underneath him, of glowing stars that disappeared in seconds. He jumped around till he was high enough near the shelves of books. I just stared at him in awe.

'It's not a dream and nor is it any nightmare,' he said. 'I'm Snow, The Guide Rabbit. And I've come here to guide you.'

'Am I going on an adventure with you?' I asked breathlessly in excitement which was being injected by the adrenaline in my bloodstream. 'A quest? And who sent you?'

'Well, you ask too many questions don't you?' Snow snapped again. He folded his limbs awkwardly which sent me into hysteric giggles suppressed by my hands. When I recovered, I saw him descend down with twinkling stars in front of me.

'So why don't you answer them?' I said, smiling widely. 'You're a guiding rabbit isn't it? Are you someone's soul?'

'I can't tell you what I actually am, but just take this that I'm here to guide you,' Snow declared with his chest puffed. 'And nobody else can see me except for you. Because I'm here for you.'

'You'll always stay here, right?'

'Yes I will. After you're gone, I'll help someone else in need.'

'Let's not talk about dying right now.'

'Okay.'

I took out my books quickly when I heard my mother's anklets clinking from the distance and began scribbling some equations I remembered. The door opened as usual and it was my mother's usual peeking from behind. After some seconds, she went away and I smiled at Snow.

'You're sneaky,' he observed.

'I've to, sometimes,' I replied. Snow sat on one of my books and looked at my equations as if he understood them. 'But I really don't believe this. I thought, everything was just fictional.'

'Writers believe in magic,' Snow said. 'Do you do that too?'

'I do, but accepting it in reality like this is difficult sometimes,' I said, balancing my pen on my index finger horizontally. 'Magic is in the air. It's everywhere around us. But what if we've lost the ability to harness it?'

'It can be.'

'What do you think?'

'I'm not a human so I don't exactly know that.'

'You're fun to talk to. I've never discussed such things with my friends. Not even with Neera.'

I scribbled some more equations and read a page or two. I still couldn't get this fact out that a rabbit from some magical world had come to guide me in my life. It was charismatic and moreover, surreal. It was something to be imagined, but it actually became my reality. I wondered if Neera would believe me if I told her about it. Of course I didn't have any proof. She'd think I'm being too imaginative.

But she won't judge me like others do. I love her for these traits.

'Totally in love with Neera, huh?' Snow said in a teasing voice.

'Weird for you, isn't it?' I smirked, doodling a rabbit at the corner of the page.

'Not for me. But you're surely going to have difficulties later on in life.'

'So are you going to guide me out of my bisexuality?'

'I don't alter with creations of God. But I do guide them to safety. For you, I know you'll fight the evils.'

'Thank you very much.'

'Send me the pictures you've taken out along with the sites.'

'Sure. Let me email them to you,' Neera replied. I could hear the shuffling of papers in her background. She surely was putting her best efforts in working with me. She knew the kind of teammate I wanted under my leadership.

'This is going to be hectic,' she whispered. 'But I won't let you regret your decision of choosing me, boss.'

'Yeah, yeah, darling.'

'Quite saying that!'

'Why?'

'Uh huh!' she snorted but I imagined her cheeks flushed red like cherries. Mine must be looking the same too. We flirted so much with each other, it almost made everyone think around us we were lesbians. Neera always laughed it out whenever I brought it. She didn't knew she always washed away my confidence of confessing about my feelings to her. I tried too often, but I never had the courage. She was another person I feared I'd lose after my family, if I was being too pushy. So I always cherry-picked my lines before saying it to her. I didn't want to be the bad guy again.

'Let's talk about work, shall we, *boss*?' Neera snapped.

'Of course.'

We did some research analysis and I explained many concepts to her. The project we're making required more of the topics related to arduino uno, and as Neera had said earlier to take the initiative, she did that. Working with AI was not my type but it typically fascinated my team partner.

Good for me. I won't have to spend hours writing the code then.

My mother came into the room while we're busy discussing. And I realized I'd forgotten to tell her about my project.

'You're *chatting?*' she shrieked like I'd brought a dead body in my room.

'No mummy, we're discussing about our science project,' I told her calmly. Neera stayed quiet and listened. 'The submission date is due on Friday this week.'

'Oh well, you could have done that afterwards,' she said, peeking at my laptop screen. She always did that to check whether I was slacking off with some videos or what. I never did. But she never believed me for it. I shrugged it off, thinking it was a natural mom instinct of keeping a check over their children's activities. 'How much time is this going to take?'

'If we work over it for the three days we've got, we'll finish it off soon,' I replied.

She looked at me and then at the list of items I'd written on a piece of paper. And then sat down on my bed behind me with her mobile phone.

'Continue with your conversation,' she said as I turned to look at her. 'And keep the phone over the speaker.'

'Why?' I asked, with a frown which disappeared as quickly as it'd come over my face when she looked at me with icy eyes, not saying anything. I turned back to my desk and put the phone over the speaker. But I kept with my research going on and stayed quiet for some time since we'd already done the discussing part and now it was time for Neera to ask her doubts while I kept looking for other topics related to the project. For some reason, mom's presence in my room was making me feel uncomfortable and letting down the suspects on me. It wasn't as if I was up to slacking off for the time being. I was working for the project.

But if you aren't doing anything wrong, then what's the big deal?

'Can you explain that topic again?' Neera's voice almost frightened me and made me flinch but my mother didn't notice it. Or she did? I couldn't dare to turn my head and look at her. That would increase fruitless suspicions. No wonder that made me look fishy.

'Which one?' I asked her.

'Wait let me see... The one involving the working of our model.'

'Sure.'

I could sense fear in her voice as well.

Why are we scared?

'What are you two working on?' mother asked in between the explanation. I stopped for a second, glancing at Snow who was seated over the notebooks and seeming much more annoyed than ever. But I told her about our project and continued.

After what felt like hours, she finally left the room and I didn't even take a second glance at the doorway. Neera must've heard her go, and I heard her let out a sigh of relief.

'The hour of terror has finally passed tonight,' she declared and I almost burst into hysterical laughter.

'Don't you say that!' I snapped but both of us giggled.

'That does suit the behaviour your mom keeps with you,' she said.

Some more hours of working and it was already one in the morning and I felt my eyelids becoming heavy. Neera was still up but she'd stopped talking ever since the clock struck past midnight. Staying up late wasn't her kind of thing, even though she'd mentioned to me that she was a night owl. I always told her she was the sun but she took the literal meaning and never understood my way of appreciation.

'Are you asleep?' I said in a low voice which had not been intended. She didn't answer and in fact, I didn't heard any rustle of paper from her side.

'Idiot,' I mumbled and yawned. The preparation to start the project was already done and it was Neera's turn to bring the items to start with her creativity. I shut down my laptop and kept the paper with diagrams and theories aside in my Chemistry book.

'Get up dummy, who'll say good night?' I said but it seemed as if she was in deep sleep. If she was, a message struck in my mind which I neither could text to her nor tell her with my ability to speak. It felt like the right time.

'I wish we stay together, forever,' I whispered, leaning over my phone. My lips almost touched the screen. 'We won't be accepted, but I'll always hold your hands until our last breaths.'

At this hour of night, I didn't know how such poetic lines were striking my brain. But whatever I said was probably not heard by Neera. I ended the call and switched off the lamp. As I proceeded towards my bed, I found something off.

I thought I kept my diary on my bed?

I looked at Snow who was already dozing off on my pillow, rolled up like a white cotton ball. His body heaved up and down slowly as he breathed.

Maybe I kept it back in the drawer.

I didn't care a look and jumped over my bed. Soon sleep came, and so did the dream.

I was in the same circus ground yet again, with the same calliope playing faintly from the tents. This time, the sound was fainter if I observed correctly. Regarding my environment and the oceanic sky with my wide eyes, I walked out at the pathway again. The band of vehicles continued to move with high speed. And on the other side far away sat Ambience with her chest puffed up.

'What do you even want?' I shouted but with all the noise of the speeding cars, she was probably not going to hear me.

Bunnies surrounded me like little butterflies around a big flower. They resembled Snow, but didn't say anything when I looked at them and just swam in the air.

Maybe I need to cross it again? But it's impossible without dying.

Without even trying, I just got jumping on the tracks, dodging the cars and buses instinctively until one of them hit me and I went into darkness.

4

The day finally came when Neera had to visit my house. Thursday hadn't been far-away; only a matter of one day for me to survive but ever since we'd talked about staying the night out while doing the project, I couldn't get the activities we were about to do off my mind. I couldn't help but imagine situations I was never going to fall into. Though we'd to work, we still could have some fun together. And maybe, it was a good chance...

'What does Neera like to eat?' mummy asked me when I sat down to have breakfast. It was the same old cereal and milk but the flavours kept changing with months. Sometimes, it was purely corn cereals, sometimes muesli and sometimes, chocolate moons if mother allowed Ava and Tarini to bring it along with other groceries from the mall.

'She likes whatever you make,' I told her. 'Anything.'

My mother didn't answer and we ate the breakfast silently. Tarini and Ava left for college soon, father went to his office and mother left for school.

'I won't be able to make anything today, but Shalini cooks food well too,' she instructed me. 'There shouldn't be any problem.'

'No mummy. We'll be fine.'

After mother left, Shalini came over and went straight to the kitchen while I waited for Neera in my room. We'd a hired cook who'd cook for us quite often and get paid for the days she'd do her job. Mother was quite busy with her work and so were Tarini and Ava, so there had to be someone to do the food-making job. I didn't mind Shalini's dishes, for they were as delicious as ever, but I did miss my mother's dishes. Soon after some months, I wouldn't even get either of the food. Just the plain old food of the mesh.

'What are your plans?' Snow asked from high above of his platform made out of cold clouds. From there, he looked like a little king of my room.

'Work for our model,' I told him while rustling papers and stuff in my bedside drawer. For some reason, I found a white chocolate wrapper with a pink heart drawn in front. Cold memories which had been burnt in the mortuary along with my older self, rose from ashes again but my new self wasn't going to make then sadden me easily.

'Looking for something?'

'Yeah, my diary... I'm pretty sure I kept it on my bed the previous night. Even then when I got to bed, I couldn't find it. I thought I'd kept in my drawer but...'

'Do you forget things often?'

I glanced at Snow and then went back to foraging my room.

'No I don't. I make sure to keep track of them because mummy tells me to be organised. And that's one rule of life as well. So why not follow it?'

'Then, do you think you misplaced your diary?'

'I'm sure I didn't.'

I searched for it more and then looked at Snow with my hands on my hips.

'Where could I have placed it?' I asked him. 'Don't you have power to find things?'

'I do, but that'll upset you here,' he replied solemnly. 'And I'm in either way not going to use it to help you.'

'You're pretty useless then I guess,' I snapped. I looked underneath the bed and even in the place where I kept my academic books and even hid candies sometimes. I never kept my personal things there because it was checked at least once in a week. So I didn't have a place to hide things for longer time.

Snow is supposed to help but he doesn't. Literally occupying my space for no good.

'Recall the events of yesterday evening,' he said.

I did. I came into my room, took out my diary to write about Snow after I discovered he was a magical rabbit and then kept it on my bed to write further during the night which was cut off from the list since I'd to do my research. In between came my mother and sat for almost an hour. Then she left and we continued till the clock had stuck past one in the morning. That's when I discovered I didn't have my diary on the bed.

A sudden chill of horror ran down my spine and through my whole body. My stomach lurched dangerously and I felt as if I'd puke but I didn't and looked down at the floor with lifeless eyes. Death was dancing in front of my vision and in fraction of seconds, I could see the drama that was going to be put up after some days or if she'd taken it with her, after some hours.

My *mother* had taken my diary.

'I'm so dead!' I said faintly with a pale face. The colours had drained out of me as I looked at myself into the mirror.

'Why?' Snow asked and I looked at him rage-filled eyes.

'WHY?' I repeated but then, lowered my voice because I wasn't home alone anymore. 'You ask why? Don't you know? My mother's going to kill me!'

'Why would she kill you?' he asked, his brows furrowed angrily.

'Because I've penned down so many my inappropriate feelings in that!' I squeaked like a mouse. I could feel my throat drying and my lips turning even drier. I was near to tears at the thought of her knowing about my sexuality and how I felt about Neera. And how I sometimes felt about my own mother's actions against me.

'Feelings aren't inappropriate,' Snow said. 'And if you know anything about privacy, you'll understand you've none of your own.'

'Why do I even need it against my own mother?' I snapped at him angrily. I felt as if that if I'll say more, I'll burst into sobs. But I didn't want to. I was not weak.

So Neera is weak? The voice in me demanded.

She's the strongest person I've met after mom.

'You do not understand,' Snow shook his little head. 'But you'll regret not setting up boundaries.'

'Rubbish,' I said and sat on my bed slowly. Goose bumps won't leave my body. I wish I hadn't made a diary in the first place. Now I understood why mom wasn't talking to me properly. I'd brought disgrace upon her.

Just then when I'd nearly lost control of my tears, I heard the doorbell ring. Shalini rushed to open it and there stood Neera at the doorway. She smiled warmly as she hopped inside, greeting Shalini warmly. She was wearing a pleated red skirt down till her ankles with heels on her feet and half red coloured shirt. Her hair was in the bun and while standing in the sun outside she looked like she'd light of her own. I sped into my room and looked at my eyes.

There they were in the sockets, red like tomatoes.

I tried to rub them and remove the redness but as soon as I heard their conversation end, I jumped to open my laptop and pretended to be busy. She opened the door and closed it behind quietly.

'Hi!' she greeted to me excitedly.

'Hi.'

'What's the matter? You look sad.'

'You just came into the room,' I snapped without looking at her. 'How can you say that?'

'I can see your eyes idiot.'

Fuck.

'Something went into it,' I said crossly. But this old method wasn't going to work in front of her. She put down the jute bag she was carrying and wrapped her hands around my neck. Her long hair caressed my face and I felt her breath on my face. It smelled of chocolate flakes.

'You're too idiot to make actual lies to me,' she whispered. 'Tell me now. Is something wrong?'

'Nothing,' I breathed. My heart beat rapidly and I feared if Neera had heard it. Her touch was enough to send me into my imaginative world. 'Let's-Let's just start the work.'

'Well, fine if you want to talk about it later.'

I nodded and she sat down on the bed, taking out all the items I'd told her to bring. Thinking my eyes had become normal, I sat on the edge of the bed and took a quick glance at Snow who was now near Neera's shoulder, looking at the items kept on the bed with great interest. She'd even brought a hard cardboard piece with her on which we were going to balance our model.

'Did I miss anything?' she asked me.

'No you brought everything.'

'Let's start with it then. Tell me the first step.'

We started but haunting thoughts never left my mind. I could only imagine my mother's angry and cold eyes on me when she'd tell me how a big disgrace I was to the family, how I'd let her down and how I would never be accepted like the way I was. These thoughts crawled into my mind and made me flinch at times. I was lost in my own world, which had become dark now. The sun had disappeared forever.

I'd always thought of revealing myself to my mother at least, thinking she would understand me, long before Ava found out about it. Don't tell mom about this, she'd warned me in a very cautious tone and even hugged me. It'd be astonishing, but soon after I found out the reason of her cautiousness. Once at the dinner table, while we're watching a movie about two lesbian girls, Tarini had brought up an innocent question of how they would have to plan about having kids. That isn't possible for them, my mother had remarked. It was true, but the way she said it was too harsh and it struck right into my heart. I stayed silent and washed away signs of any suspicious emotion on my face. Of course, she was homophobic, like others were. Except for Ava, Tarini and Neera. I didn't know about my father. But her reaction had instilled fear inside me for sure. And too sacred to tell anyone else more about it, I wrote a good three pages about it in my diary, with *special* colourful pens making the page vibrant. 'IT'S NOT A CHOICE, IT'S GOD'S PLAN' I'd written in big bold letters. And now she was going to read all of it. She was going to know how disgraceful her daughter was.

DISGRACE

Secondly, many pages had penned thoughts of the days when she was too rude to me for no reasons and I wrote them down to satisfy my anger. Those were her worthless arguments with me. But deep down, I knew she was not going to forgive me. Never.

'TARA!' Neera shouted in my ears and I gasped loudly, flinching back and vibrating like a guitar string for a second. I looked at her with heavy breaths as she stared at me with confused eyes.

'What?' I seethed, calming my heart down with gentle rubs on my chest. Neera frowned, but she had worry in her voice.

'You're lost somewhere else,' she said. 'Now you better tell me what happened.'

'Just do your work and don't intervene,' I snapped angrily at her. Her eyes changed noticeably and widened but her lips remained parted and no words came out. I was really upset with her behaviour. Couldn't she just leave me alone for a second?

I left the room to get a glass of water and almost bumped into Shalini who was carrying a glass filled with cold drink. I didn't match my gaze with her as she proceeded towards my room.

I need to calm down.

But adrenaline rushed through my body and made my hands shake a little as I reached for the RO tap. Horror had struck me like my exam results whenever I failed to get the required percentage. And if I explained to Neera about it, I would surely break down.

You cannot. You're not weak.

I took a sip which increased the discomfort in my stomach even more but my dry throat needed it. I looked at the clock while returning to my room.

11:15 AM

Only few hours before I face my wrath.

I entered the room quietly and sat down beside her with my laptop on my lap. The job of making the presentation was mine. And I'd to focus on it. Neera didn't poke me and didn't even give me a side glance. I expected her to, but why was I even expecting in the first place?

I instructed her to work properly and not make a mess out of the tissue papers dipped in Fevicol liquid mixed with little amount of water. The cardboard she'd brought was tougher than I'd thought and it was going to require many coatings of tissue paper before she actually started painting it. I selected designs for the presentation and showed it to her at times, before starting to work on one slide and after finishing off with it.

'Sir Anthony said that we'd have to speak on it as well and not just email the presentation to him,' Neera told her. Her voice sounded casual, but I knew she wasn't going to talk to me until I was fine myself. Which I surely wasn't going to for a month at least.

'That's no problem,' I said. 'I'll give you your lines and the rest, I'll handle it. Any other conditions?'

'Nothing. Just do the same if the model gets selected. But for parents, he has asked to use a simple explanation and not the brute one which we understand in lessons.'

'Not a big deal.'

Soon enough, covering the cardboard was done and it was lunch time. Shalini had prepared bean stripes with potatoes (Barbatti) and rotis. She served us and herself took some and sat down on the floor.

'Why do you sit on the floor?' I asked her once when I was around eleven. She smiled, a wide grin on her wheat-coloured chubby face and answered me.

'When we sit on the floor to have lunch, we connect ourselves to the earth. And moreover, it improves our pachan kriya.'

'Why don't you let me sit on the floor to have food?' I asked my mother. She looked at me, and then glanced at Shalini who looked down at her plate. But she didn't scoff like she usually did.

'You don't need to, and we've table to have food on,' she replied.

'But then, why don't you make Shalini sit with us?'

There was something in her eyes then which I couldn't understand at that time. Probably guilt, or something much bigger than my vocabulary of words. But whatever it was, it did killed my curiosity instantly and I realised I'd crossed the line of interrogating my own mother.

'Finish you lunch quickly and go to bed,' she said with the same coldness. I nodded and hurriedly ate my dinner to avoid her line of sight from me.

I glanced at our maid, who'd worked for us since I was little, and then back at my food. Whatever reasons she'd for sitting on the floor traced the roots of our Indian culture. I wondered if my mother agreed with Shalini and let her sit on the floor, or was she just ignorant? I couldn't think. I didn't *dare* to think.

We ate our food in complete silence, while Shalini finished earlier than us and then moved out into the blistering summer heat to attend a phone call. I couldn't match my gaze with Neera, nor look at her plate as to how much she'd finished. But instead, I felt her leg rest on mine sideways and my heart paced even faster.

'What's the matter, Tara?' she said in the warmest tone I'd ever heard from her, and for a moment, it became hard to even swallow the bolus I'd in my neck. I thought I'd break down yet again. But I didn't. I didn't even answer her.

She didn't force me. But I didn't want her to be worried about me.

'I'm on my periods,' I lied to her. The best way to describe the meanness I'd shown to her. The beast of my side which almost came out.

'Oh silly, so you're on *that* part of the month,' she smiled at me but I didn't match gaze with her. My heart was becoming heavier with her words. It was a limbo in which I'd fallen. I knew I shouldn't have done that, but I still did. 'I've some chocolates. Your favourite candies. Why didn't you tell me before? Should I massage your shoulders?'

'No I'm fine.'

'Then what can I do to lighten your mood? Kiss you?'

I looked at her with surprise and we burst into giggles. I almost chocked on my food and had to drink water to avoid bursting my oesophagus. But I kind of wished she was serious about it.

'You can if you want,' I said with a sly smile and she elbowed me in the ribs.

'You romantic nerd,' she laughed out pleasantly with her red cheeks lifted up to support the smile on her face. 'You're always flirting with me like I'm you girlfriend or something.'

'Would you like to become then? To justify the flirting?'

We looked at each other dumbfounded. I didn't know how such flirty lines even came up from my throat and used the air to travel out of my lips without thinking. Here I was about to be cooked, but I still had the same attitude with her. But even for the split seconds before Shalini entered and locked the door behind which broke our gazes like glass, I could feel the warmth on my lips come back. I could feel part of me jumping with dopamine and screaming at the touch of our legs. But the moment didn't last for long and we looked down at our hands. I imagined myself red like a cherry.

'I'll wash the plates,' Shalin said but I'd suddenly got the energy to do everything in the house.

'It's fine, I'll do it,' I said to her. 'Please rest for a while.'

'*Malkin* hasn't allowed for it,' the lady said with nervousness and terror.

'I'm the daughter,' I said, smiling. Behind her, I saw Neera smile as well. 'And it's no big deal.'

We returned back to our room, but something new had blossomed in between us. I felt it and I knew she felt it too. But I didn't mention it.

'He messaged you yet again?' I exasperated and she nodded. 'Why don't you just block him off?'

'I'm observing him for now,' she replied, opening her phone lock. She showed me all the chats they'd been having. And Swastik always messaged at night. When it was my time to message her.

'What a jerk!' I snarled at the texts as if they actually had Swastik's face. 'Just block him already. He gets on my nerves every time you mention him. And I don't like it when he takes you away from me at the night.'

'Oh dear, you hate him with all your core,' Neera giggled at my puffed face. 'And I'm yours anyway. I won't be of someone else. Never.'

'Whatever,' I snorted, trying to drive off the blush warming my cheeks. 'What else does he try to say?'

'He kind of is on the verge of actually proposing to me,' she said and I looked at her with a I-knew-it-all-from-the-beginning gaze. 'Let's see what he actually does. I can't say much about it.'

'Using the same trick to attract butterflies to his web,' I snorted, typing furiously. I'd prepared three slides till now, along with the dialogues scribbled in the spiral bound notebook beside me. 'But he thinks he can attract a dragoness there.'

'Aye! Thanks for calling me a dragoness,' Neera said, smiling. 'But whatever he's planning, I'll not fall for it. He thinks he'll manipulate me against you.'

'Not happening.'

The fear in me had drained and I felt I could face the wrath a little less painfully, now that I'd Neera with me.

Mummy won't scold me in front of her, would she? She knows it destroys me. She won't do it, would she?

It was five in the evening. Tarini and Ava rushed into the house and greeted Neera while I was almost half-asleep while working on the PPT. I usually took naps in the afternoon for thirty to forty five minutes to recharge my system (I referred myself as a robot for some reason), but Neera being there didn't let me do so. We talked a lot while working, and half of the model had already been finished; at least the skeleton was done.

'Hi!' Tarini flashed a big grin at her. I tried to remember if she ever did that to me. Ava glanced at me notoriously and I flustered furiously. If I'd to hide myself I would've done that.

'We've brought some snacks along with us, come and eat,' Ava said and they took Neera out of the room even after her polite denials. I looked at the doorway dumbfounded, like I didn't even existed at that time.

Snow hopped down to me. I'd totally forgotten about him.

'Are you hungry? Where have you been this whole time?' I asked him.

'I don't eat but the carrots were really good,' he snickered. 'I was watching you two from the Moons.'

'So you went to the Moon to watch how I flustered when Neera touched me every time?' I smiled.

'Not *Moon*. It's *Moons*. The rabbits of share three of their own moons.'

'That's just like my storyline. I wish I could work on it.'

'You can, but you know why you can't.'

'I do.'

I stretched my arms and back and walked out with the rabbit sitting on top of my head like he owned a priced possession. Tarini and Ava had brought momos with them and they were feasting on it. Neera passed me a guilty look while she chewed on the vegetable-filled momos. She knew I was forbidden to have them.

'They contain some things which aren't good for health,' my mother had instructed. 'And the layer is made of *maida*. It's not even nutritious for you.'

'I've brought boba tea for you,' Tarini said and patted gently on the small paper bag beside her. 'Reusable cup. Five pouches. Chocolate flavoured.'

'Wow, I thought I didn't even live here,' I retorted at her grinning face. I took the packet out of the paper bag. It was gorgeous from the outside, with the plastic cup etched with beach scenery and five pouches inside. I took it to the kitchen and prepared two glasses of boba with the shiny tapioca pearls. I had drank it only once from a stall near our school, and it did taste amazing with the stretchy balls.

'Thank you for this,' Neera smiled, once we got back into our room. Ava was interested in seeing our model so she came in with us.

'This is a great idea,' she nodded thoughtfully. 'When is this going for submission?'

'Friday,' Neera said.

'Hey, I heard you'll be staying over tonight, isn't it?' my sister looked at Neera with glittering eyes. I immediately got reminded of Prasanna, of how she teased me whenever Neera was around. Initially, it'd been a brutal teasing when I'd first become her friend. Being a newly admitted student in grade eight, she didn't talk much but she soon joined our small group. She smiled much often and I kept falling head over heels for her.

As I thought about those moments, I realized I'd already become a disgrace to my family. Loving someone from the same gender as me, not bringing the ideal marks, not ready to give up my passion for writing. I couldn't turn the time back and in some way, I didn't want to. I didn't want to lose the gift of writing that I'd received from God. The art of storytelling which I possessed was hated by my mother, ever since I opposed their idea of cracking either JEE or NEET. I'd no choice. Be disgraceful until I did what they wanted, not break their chains... and leave Neera. I was in between the balance of choices. Take one and move forward.

Be successful, mother's voice rang in my head. *Only then will everyone see you with respect.*

I know that, a ten year old me replied while sitting on her lap. *I know I will. I'll never let you down.*

You never will, she smiled. *I've raised you with goodness. Walk only on the right path. I'll always be there to guide you.*

Guilt struck me like a knife.

I've let her down. I'm disgrace.

But you still have time to fix things, it's not late, something spoke up.

What can I do?

Anything that disappoints them, you need to leave that. Simple.

Is it really simple?

Yes it is. You're a champion, Tara. You don't need anyone's guidance except for your mother. And all this bisexuality is just nonsense. You're on the wrong path. When she'll come she'd tell you the right path.

But I'm scared of the judgements.

It's only a matter of time. You've lost yourself. But you can only get back to where you belong only by leaving this mind-set. You were never like this before.

I know but-

No 'buts'. Try to recall who you were...

I blinked at Neera and my sister immersed in talking to each other about school, friends, and me. As if she was setting up our marriage.

'What do you like to eat?' Ava asked her. 'We'll order some food according to your wish tonight.'

'She doesn't eat junk food like you two do,' I snapped.

'You know a lot, huh?' Ava asked in a mischievous tone and I struggled to keep off the redness from reaching my cheeks.

No! Keep in control.

'Fish Scales! Come here!' Tarini shouted from outside and my sister sighed, rolling her eyes. Neera looked at us for a moment and then switched her gaze towards me for an answer.

'That's her name,' I explained. 'Because she likes fish more than chicken meat.'

'And you could've just *not* told the entire history!' Ava snapped at me like a snapper fish. But she could say no more as Tarini's burning gaze filled the room.

'What a mess you've made on my bed!' she snarled. 'Clean it before I complain to mom!'

'FINE!' Ava growled and jumped up. After she left, I was back to my senses and the judgements I'd been making with myself. Neera stared at the model kept in front of her, with its paper bins attached on the vibrant blue sheet of paper. Much of the part was done, but it was still going to take another few hours to be complete.

'I feel sleepy now,' she yawned and stretched her hands above, the soft sounds of bones snapping in her vertebrae and hand joints. She jerked her head sideways and rubbed her eyes lazily, almost wanting to keep them rubbing forever and see the galaxies one saw when they did that. But she dropped her hands on her lap and blinked with her wide eyes. While I watched the simplest act of stretching shown by the most beautiful person on earth for me, I forgot everything I'd explained to myself and simply embraced myself with her love. She looked at me and after three whole seconds, I looked down at my laptop screen stupidly.

'Is something wrong?' Neera asked, edging towards me. Her perfume scent lingered in my nose, teasing me dangerously but I shook my head violently, confusing her more and inviting trouble myself.

'Nothing,' I said, covering my face.

Gosh! I don't even know what I'm doing.

'You're all shy and timid all of a sudden,' she subdued. 'Totally like a bunny washing his face.'

'I don't even act like you, yet she thinks all bunnies do that,' Snow puffed his face as I looked at him on Neera's shoulder. Following my gaze, she looked over her shoulder but then at me, puzzled. Till then, I'd my eyes set on her to avoid suspicion.

'Is something there over my shoulder?' she asked, touching her ear gently.

'No.'

'You're being strange.'

'No, I'm not.'

'Yes you're.'

'No.'

She narrowed her eyes and to avoid that, I continued working on the PPT. And fortunately, Anya's call interrupted the hectic situation.

'Hi Tara, are you busy?' she asked. I put the phone on speaker so that Neera could hear, even though she asked me not to. What was the problem?

'Yeah, we're working on the project right now.'

'Oh! Well, what are you guys working on?'

'I can't tell you that.'

There was a moment of silence, as if Anya hadn't expected that from me. But I'd the answers ready with me for such situations, as my mother had taught me to. I was just going to run over the same macros again in my system.

'I'm not going to steal it! We've started with our own project now,' she laughed it off.

'If you've done so, why do you want to know about mine? What good will it do to you?'

Another moment of silence.

'Fine. Could you just email me your PPT so that I can take some inspirations?'

'Absolutely not.'

Neera opened her mouth a couple of times and closed it, reaching out to touch my arm but I was not going to let this slide of easily.

'I said I'm *not* going to steal!' Anya stretched in a long drawl. 'I just want to take a look!'

'But I don't want you to, and that's my choice. Why should I reveal my plans before the main event?'

'So you don't trust your friends?'

'This has nothing to do with my hard work. In fact, *our* hard work. We're working so much for this, and I'm definitely not going to make the dumb mistake of sharing the details of my project to anyone. Even with my own closest friends.'

'You know what? You're just arrogant! Being a valedictorian has made your one!'

'I don't care!' I snapped angrily and Neera flinched. I didn't look at her unless I'd cut Anya's call. Then, softening my gaze I glanced at our model and at her, expecting her to scold me. But instead, she was proud or maybe worried, or both.

'I'd to, or else she would have not listened,' I said to her. 'I'm not going to trust anyone with the project. Not that they can't be trusted, but with the intention that the world is not the same anymore.'

'Your mother's lines,' my best friend nodded. 'They're effective. And useless. But always make sure to use them at the right place. As for Anya, she shouldn't have said that...'

'I've the habit of listening to it now,' I replied casually. 'That's what they all say.'

Because they don't know what I've to deal with. Even if they did, they would only make fun of it.

This reminded me of the poem we'd studies in standard ten; *Atmakatha* by Jaishankar Prasad absolutely told the truth about the reality of people. You thought you could share your worries with everyone to get sympathy and they would show it in the front but behind the back, they'll only judge you and make fun of you. I didn't want that. Plus, sharing about your insecurities wasn't a very good idea in the first place. The world is not the same anymore.

'I don't,' Neera smiled and I smiled back, only to get pulled down my thoughts again.

Don't.

I heard the doorbell ring again, and even if it could've been my father, I was pale with fear. The colour must've drained out of my face, because Neera's smile disappeared after looking at me. All the lurching that had been going inside my stomach now almost made me hurl out everything, so to suppress that, I drank some water with an emotionless and white face.

'What happened?' Neera jerked me after I was done. 'You really need to stop hiding this Tara. Please tell me what's up?'

I could've passed a joke for her last sentence, but it wasn't a good situation to do that. I heard the sound of those dominating anklets walk into the living room and the door close being her. I heard the creaking of our old couch bought a few years ago made from the excellent wood of mahogany as she slouched on it like she always did. I could hear her voice ordering Tarini to give her some water. Tarini's excited storytelling began soon after handing her the water; about her college and her band about to give another performance next month. Sounds of appreciation could be heard from the dragoness on the couch. Then came Ava's voice, as she brought her project grades to her. Again, appreciations.

I'm going to report her soon.

Then the couch creaked again and the anklets clinked towards my room. Before I could prepare myself, the door opened and in came the coldness along with her. I flinched a little and became stiff. Neera's greeting game me some moments to collect myself.

'I'm so glad you're here,' my mother said cheerfully.

She's so mad. I can already sense it.

They exchanged their well-beings for minutes and then, after inspecting our model, she left the room. She didn't even glance at me. Not even once.

I'm already done.

Neera excused herself to use the washroom and I looked at Snow who came hopping towards me.

'You've yet to understand many things,' he said, touching my cheeks with his paws.

'I don't know that,' I said faintly. 'But I sure do know what's going to happen next.

5

The auditorium of the school was absolutely massive than the other structures present around. It rose around almost high above the two wings of the school, towering and standing at the edge of the stone path leading to the old wing. The two pillars that went up to form a gable roof with the school's logo, slogan and the famous Sanskrit lines 'Vasudhaiva Kutumbakam' stuck with golden words underneath the shackles. There were four entrances, the main one having a small corridor or glass wall and a huge mural of Madhubani art hung in a protected glass frame on other wall. A small stair on the left lead to the gallery view of the stage, but it was never used by any students, probably because it wasn't even allowed to use that entrance as it was opened only for parents during 'Prize Nite' or other occasions, but never for students. Other two entrances faced the stones path, connected to the outer corridor of the auditorium where students who danced would sometimes come to practice, lovers would come to talk length of their promises and the singers would rarely use for practicing their vocals. Usually, they got the stage for themselves or the green rooms but if they didn't or the auditorium was locked, they would take place in the corridors behind the grills and the huge potted lemon grass leaves. Inside, on occasions, the students were made to sit on the check-board like tiles in hues of mahogany red and cream but they mostly hated it because most of the times, the floor was covered with slight traces of ground mud. The length stretched across to connect the glass door entrance of the back and if six classes were called at the same time, they would be pushed back to sit behind. The fourth entrance was on the left side or the left narrower passage where the toilets and the gardening tools were present. The three entrances served as emergency exits for calamities, as was always announced in safety tips whenever elocutions took place.

The high ceiling that rose up and up had fall ceiling of a darker shade of peach with little spot lights embedded in them like small planets casting light. The warmer lights were present on the side walls high above the jute acoustic panels, and the only time I'd seen them switch was on my tenth Prize Nite. The stage in front had a white screen behind it, as most of the events required slide shows, like ted talks, elocutions, story-telling and many others.

Right now, it was being used as an exhibition of the science fest.

'Make sure you explain properly and avoid jargon,' the science teachers explained to us. We'd been told to come earlier than the parents, obviously to make sure our model wasn't damaged while being kept in the school labs. Rows of tables had been kept at alternate lines of squares with models and model numbers.

'This feels exciting,' Neera bubbled to her neighbour Nayani who nodded at us. She had made her team with Anya, who didn't even look at us for once when we came to our model beside them. I didn't care much but Neera glanced at us for a couple of times, though she said nothing about it.

They had made a working sensor powered by the light which would be casted on the solar panel and move according to the light. The model was clean and looked good and I wondered why Anya was even worrying about our model in the first place. Hers looked better than ours. But in terms of the modular decoration Neera had done, ours was better.

I placed my laptop in front of me and went through the PPT once to check if any misfortune of a disappearing slide had happened. Everything was fine. I turned it around so it faced the people who were going to see our models. Neera fished out her little slip of lines I'd drafted for her and read it once in a whispered tone. For myself, I was going to improvise and show-off my public speaking skills.

'How are we going to understand if they understood or not?' Neera asked me. 'That's the main purpose right?'

'I don't actually care if someone understands or not, to be honest,' I yawned. 'Because I've prepared the speech and the PPT using the simplest words I could find to replace with the harder ones. And we don't need to think about that. The main judges are the special guests. So we should focus on being more prim and proper while explaining to them. And as we noticed in the previous exhibitions, parents are not really interested in explanations and some only want to see the models working.'

'Alright, so we've to kind and good here.'

'Of course, that's *obvious* you know.'

'Okay, don't get heated up. You're worried about the Physics grades aren't you?'

I fiddled with my ID card while looking straight in front where chemical bottles, heart, lungs, atoms, earth and solar system had been made from polystyrene to decorate the stage where we'd be given prizes after a few days of the decision. Of course I was tensed. And who wasn't going to be? Oh well, they weren't expecting *me* to be tensed, and I understood it perfectly even more than I understood my own feelings sometimes.

'You worry a lot about your marks,' Nayani said. But her tone sounded cruel to me. *Shouldn't I worry?* 'You know you'll score well and yet you continue with your drama every time.'

'Well average students can never understand a valedictorian's position, so it'd be better if you just shut that mouth of yours,' I said in the most calm tone I could find inside me throat and that literally made Nayani and Anya's eyes turn wide. Even Neera looked at me but there was a little amusement in her eyes.

'I don't understand why she talks like this!' Anya scoffed angrily, looking at me with a disgust. 'You're really arrogant!'

'The audacity she has!' Nayani gasped. 'I didn't expect this from you! What's wrong with you?'

'If you think I've god-gifted senses of scoring well, get your brains checked,' I said again and just turned away when Shashank called me to his model for a second. I could hear them arguing Neera while my best friend handled the situation. Prasanna was also there with Shashank and she looked over my shoulder at the cat fight going on in whispers.

'What's up with that argument there?' she asked me.

'Nothing, they were just praising how good I was,' I said, shrugging my shoulders as to indicate that I didn't even want to talk about it.

'Tara, you look tired,' Shashank observed with his black eyes behind the thin-rimmed spectacles. He was the one boy I talked to about almost everything (Not what went in my house) and we even had those flirting talks sometimes in between if I took leave from my dignity for some seconds. But above all, he was that protective brother best friend I, Neera, Prasanna and our other best friend Tanuj admired the most. In fact, we had our secret group which excluded Neera since she was 'too innocent' for our conversation, but the fact that she never got jealous made me sometimes suspect if she was the perfect girl everyone was looking for. And sadly, I couldn't get her.

'Your eyes look all tired and sleepy,' he said. 'Like us.'

'They do?' I asked and rubbed my eyes. But rubbing them did make sleep come to me and it felt like a mistake. I looked at my watch. Still had time to wash my face and come back again.

'You look as if you didn't even have a wink of sleep last night,' Prasanna said. 'I've a chocolate bar. It'll give you some energy.'

'No, Neera already has my supplies ready,' I smiled at them.

'That girl with specs?' Shashank asked, pointing at the angel who had somehow calmed the duo I'd made incensed with her outstandingly kind skills. Sometimes, I wish I was a better person like her. Then, mother would've loved me more.

'Her girlfriend,' Prasanna mumbled behind my back as she came to my side and my heart leapt, thinking Shashank had heard it but he looked at the two of us; me who was almost strangling Prasanna and her who was giggling like maniac while saving herself. But now that they'd mentioned it, I could feel pain in my shoulders and leg joints and the dullness of the vision. I'd had my breakfast but the thought of the day ending soon and hugging my bed began wandering in my head. I returned back to my table and thankfully Neera was on my left, acting as a barrier between the two girls who'd stepped into my 'just classmates' list from that time onwards.

'Can you attend me to the washroom with me?' I asked her. 'Just for a moment?'

'Of course,' she said. She glanced at the model and I called out to Shashank.

'Would you mind taking care of our model and laptop while we come from the washroom?' I asked and he gave me a thumbs-up. 'Just in case, the so called "movie accidents" happen.'

The last line was lower in tone but assuming the auditorium was only full of whispers and the two of them listening to all my talks to Neera thinking I would waste my precious time in discussing about them. We exited the cold air-conditioned auditorium and proceeded towards the washroom of the old wing. On our way, I was caught by our Hindi lecturer. And the usual tasks were assigned; of bringing the papers at the end of the day to be shown before the report card.

'Now don't start again with your questions,' I warned Neera while wiping my face as she opened her mouth to say something after observing me. 'Before I get angry for that, I just want to say that I'm not in a good mood.'

'Okay, I won't,' she said calmly. A lot of things had messed up my mind and I was absolutely not going to ruin myself after yelling at Neera for small things. 'Do you want chocolates?'

'Not now.'

'A hug?'

'No.'

'Well, well, Ms. Tara Saini,' Neera smiled, folding her arms as I gave her a side-eyed look. I kept my handkerchief in my pocket. 'You know you can tell me everything. Even if something's bothering you, I'll help you out.'

I left the washroom with her without saying anything. She followed me behind and thankfully, with God's grace, she didn't ask me for an answer because I would've broken down in front of her.

'I know your mother is not talking to you,' she said from behind me, but that didn't stop to look at her dramatically. I knew she knew. I knew she knew it because she observed everything in that night's stay. I knew she knew everything because I wanted her to. I didn't want to declare it, but she knew I hated it. She knew everything.

My mother hated me. I knew it. Neera didn't accept it.

The exhibition went well and ended around half past twelve. Since the summer timing for dispersal was one past forty, we still had time to get our answer sheets for a day to be shown to the parents and bring them back the next day. Even a circular had been sent to the online class group where the announcements came, so the students don't fool their parents. But still, they could find other ways. And I couldn't.

I'd asked Snow to stay at house but he'd urged to follow me to my school just to see if the classroom walls of the junior students had rabbits painted on them. And after the exhibition ended, he hoped back to me and stayed around, inspecting the students of my class with beady eyes. I wanted to stroke him, but that would look stupid and creepy for others, as if I was stroking the empty air. Snow and I'd become best friends over time and I even saw him in that one dream which had Ambience on the other side, always staring and always judging me. I tried to decode what it meant and if it was connected to some mystery like they showed in the movies and wrote in the novels, but I only died in my dreams. I was stuck.

The papers came and I saw the grades I got.

CHEMISTRY: 70
PHYSICS: 75
MATHEMATICS: 73
HINDI: 78
ENGLISH: 70
PHYSICAL EDUCATION: 72

Not good. How will I even show these marks to her?
I calculated the percentage and even interrogated the salutatorian and the other good students who actually never paid much attention to the ranks.

PERCENTAGE: 93%

I stared at the calculations. And I did them again. I did them again and again and with each steps my heart sank and the colours drained from my body. It almost frightened Neera, whatever I was doing and tearing the page with the hard grip of my pen on it.

I didn't work for this. I deserved more! How did it come to this?
'And once again, Tara has topped the class again!' the class teacher announced and everyone clapped. But behind the fake smile that was painted on my face forever, I felt the disgraceful looks of my parents. Behind the fake sound of claps were the whispers of envy. I liked the taste of envy

that others felt. At least, that coped me up and didn't make me feel all useless.

As I was getting back to my seat, my chemistry teacher called me out of the class. I thought it was some another work before the day ended for us, but what she said next devastated my leftover confidence completely.

'I expected more from you in my subject at least,' she said, trying to sound normal but the tone gave away her annoyance. 'But I know you can do better. If you have any problem in future, call me. Or you can even message me.'

I nodded, shocked at her words but I didn't show it. After the school ended and I walked out of the classroom, forgetting to wait for Neera, I thought I would burst then and there itself.

I'm working so hard. Only to listen to such disappointed feedbacks? Why do they not understand what I'm going through? I'm not a machine. What is the use of working so hard then?

'Hey, congrats,' Neera greeted me but I didn't even give her a look. I paced out of the busy corridor, almost losing her in the crowd of students, some blaming the teachers for not giving them marks or cutting their marks purposely while some promising their friends to work harder for the next term.

'Oi! Tara!' I heard Neera's shouts which drowned in the noise of the crowd and I walked out without giving her another look. But she caught up to me and turned me around to face her. I almost got knocked off by a huge fat boy moving around.

'Just leave me!' I snarled at her angrily.

'What's wrong with you?' she snapped back. Her chest heaved up and down, as if she'd suffocated in the crowd inside. There were beads of sweat lining her forehead, from the hurried task Sir Victor had given her of climbing to the second floor and fetching his bag from the ATL lab.

'If you'll just leave me, nothing will go wrong!' I growled. 'You worry too much for no reason!'

'Then what about your tone?' she cried. I rolled my eyes and turned to leave but she wouldn't leave my hand.

'Just leave me I said. You don't respect someone's boundaries!'

'I do. But you've been suffering and I won't let you suffer!'

'I hate you.'

She blinked at me a couple of times. We'd found a quiet corner to have our argument and it was irritating me. Everything was irritating me. I didn't have the slightest energy to fight anymore.

'What?' she asked faintly.

'*I hate you*!' I repeated, stressing each word in my sentence. Tears were starting to emerge to the brink of my eyelids. 'I hate your kindness. I hate how you're always perfect in morals. I hate it when I see you're the more compatible daughter. *I hate it when you care for me!*'

Neera opened her mouth to speak but a lump was forming in my throat. So I jerked away her grip and walked away.

I HATE MYSELF.

6

The final day of the report card came, and so came the time when I was about to get the worst scolding of my life ever. While I was busy brushing my hair in the morning, I happened to chance upon my parents' room and found my diary in my mother's closet as I was searching for my new pair of socks she'd bought a few months ago. I knew she'd taken it, but I couldn't believe the fact that she was so interested in reading the hundred pages of my thoughts and anxious worries. As I came to think to file all my thoughts into a single folder and name it, I found I couldn't. There were already separate folders available for each on them, some of them whose directory route had been lost and some which still thrived in the desktop. Somewhere, all of this was leading to a conclusion upon analysing each folder and file, but that conclusion was still taking time to be downloaded.

I took it back to my room and began searching for a good place to hide it. Honestly, I was scared at the beginning because of how I'd no privacy of my own and how I couldn't keep a diary. And I thought of either burning it or throwing it. I wasn't supposed to be second-thinking my mom's commands and what she told me. I was the one at fault for thinking they were wrong. She was only trying to bring me to the right path. To remove some part of my guilt, I'd even stopped talking to Neera at night.

'You're so confused,' Snow shook his head with disappointment. I narrowed my eyes at him wrathfully and continued with my hunt for a new place. If I hid it in Tarini's room, precisely in her closet, mother won't even care to look into it because she didn't have even patience to forage through her hundred clothes. And if I hid it in Ava's messy room where the papers were always scattered with hauntingly beautiful art and several devices on her bed, she would definitely think I hid my diary there because of how messy Ava's room was. Analysing her mind-set about me, she would think I wouldn't chose Tarini's clean room, but with time, I knew her better as her third daughter.

'Decided. I'm going to hide this in Tarini's closet,' I turned to Snow. 'I'm already doomed. But I'll find a way to burn this.'

'Burn all your emotions, all your memories?' he asked. I nodded.

'The memories it contains are not worth remembering,' I said, sighing. 'They'll only hurt me much more and remind me of the times when I was miserable and when I wasn't a good daughter. And now, even if mom stops talking to me for a year to punish me, I'll accept it and happily learn the lesson.'

'Well Tara, I think she has other plans,' Snow rolled over his back and let me rub his belly while he closed his eyes. 'She can't be this cruel to you just for some marks and for some opinions where you are right with your thought process.'

'You have been stalking her or something?' I asked him.

'I can see everyone in the house,' he replied, rolling over and kissing on my nose. I loved it when he did that, and

I loved him too much. With time, I'd realised that Snow didn't need any food to live because of his special powers but I still shared my snacks with him. And I always had that feeling of the special girl who had her special magical rabbit. Not to mention that he rarely used his skills for guiding me. The other day, I almost fell into the drain while focusing on examining my nails.

'That's called stalking,' I said. 'And today, you'll come with me to get the report card as well.'

'Okay.'

I took a peek in the living room before leaving my own room and sped into Tarini's room, almost making her gasp in surprise.

'Shush!' I whispered, keeping a finger on my lips. She was in her crème coloured shirt and dark grey skirt, preparing for her college. Her hair was on her shoulder like brown waterfalls catching the light from the window, curled at the lower ends like waves. Sometimes, I wondered if she faked that she didn't have lovers mad behind her, or she just didn't want to take compliments from me.

'What the hell are you up to?' she whispered back in a strained voice. 'That's not how you enter someone's room! I'm your elder sister!'

'Morals aside, I need your help,' I said, bringing up the diary to her face. She looked at it but didn't take it from me. 'I need to hide this in your closet for some time while I find a way to burn it.'

'Why? What does it have?'

'Nothing, it's just my diary.'

'You want to burn your diary? And on top of that, you want to burn a *diary*?'

'Yes.'

'How did you come to the terms of burning a book?' she demanded, not in the mood for jokes. 'Wasn't that a sin for writers and you said you'd be sent to *narak* after your inevitable death?'

I opened my mouth but I couldn't say anything. Of course, it was a *sin* for writers at least to *treat* a *book* like that! What was I even thinking?

The demon has taken over my mind, I guess.

'Alright then, help me hide this in your closet,' I demanded. 'Mummy won't find it there, right?'

'She can, but she finds it irritating to search my closet,' Tarini replied as a matter of fact. 'But, but. She can still think of this trick and search it nonetheless. I know a better place for it.'

She opened her cabinet piled with books of accountancy and banking and question banks, some on the threat of falling down on her study table and one actually did; Tarini caught it mid-air and it almost gave me a heart attack because if mother would've heard it, she would've obviously come to check. And 'me' being in Tarini's room was quite fishy for her. Instead of this, I was supposed to get ready for my report card meeting. And here I was, sulking around with my stupid diary which got me in trouble in the first place.

'Give it to me.'

I handed the diary to her and she stood on her heels to put it behind some old books whose covers had white lines scratching the design and torn corners. She put some more books covering the behind and finally, the setup looked like it hadn't been touched in a while.

'There, nobody touches that except for me,' Tarini said, dusting her hands. 'It'll always be safe in there. But tell me, why are you trying to hide it? Isn't it already safe in your room?'

'Mummy took it two months ago and since then she hasn't been talking to me,' I explained to her. Now that I was ready to accept my faith, I said it with ease. No lumpy throats, no lurching stomachs. But the reaction Tarini gave was full of distaste.

'She *read* your diary?' she shrieked and I jumped to silence her again. 'Tara, that is not acceptable at all! You know it's like invading your privacy!'

'Not you talking about privacy too!' I groaned. 'It was my fault to keep a diary in the first place. And I'm not supposed to be thinking all wrong things and writing them down too.'

'Bro are you serious?' she squeezed her eyes and gave me a disdainful look.

'I'm your *sister*,' I grinned at her but that didn't bring a smile on her face.

'Stop that, you're not seeing the seriousness of this situation,' she said sternly. 'Do you even have the slightest idea of how this can affect your future? I'm not saying against mom but this is not acceptable at all.'

'How does that even matter?' I asked.

But before she could reply, I was called by mummy in the living room for the breakfast. Tarini shook her head in disappointment and muttered something under her breath which I couldn't understand. I went to have breakfast and mother didn't even have the slightest care to ask me what I'd been doing in Tarini's room. I sat beside Ava and fed on the chocolate moons. Tarini later joined me but she wouldn't even look at me, as if she was disgusted in some way.

After the duo left and father went to work, mother took out the car and we drove on our way to school silently.

I remained stiff as a log on my seat, thinking even one movement could let her know my presence in the car while she focused on the road. It was strange how we did that as kids, thinking we would become invisible if we remained unmoving and lifeless and it had become so habitual to me that I did it even now, though I was close to becoming a young adult soon in November.

The traffic filled road reminded me of the dream and how I'd progressed a little in that. I could reach half-way towards Ambience and the dragoness did absolutely nothing to help me. This traced to the last time I'd seen her sketch again, around some few months ago.

Snow sat on my lap while I looked out through my side window. I'd expected my mother to not talk to me, and why would she do that? I'd not fulfilled her wish and in no way was I going to be treated friendly. But she did, almost making me flinch.

'Where's you designated class located at?' she asked me. I glanced her a hurried look. She didn't look at me.

'It's on the first floor in the old wing,' I replied.

'Great. I won't have to climb the stairs then.'

Recently, she complained a lot about her knee joints paining and found out it was because of the uric acid that had formed there. Calcium and magnesium pills had been bought, but she relied mostly on the ayurvedic remedies. At least, I was satisfied that she hadn't stopped applying the remedies on me. The two of us were the only ones in the house who gladly accepted the bitterest tastes and yet drank the worst health drinks ever to keep fit but it was a linking chain. Maybe, she didn't hate me totally.

'Is Neera coming in this time slot or hers is different?

'She must've taken her card already. Hers was before me.'

'Oh, very well.'

'No mother hates her children,' Snow sang out. I kept petting him gently to keep the anxiety away. I'd told her about my percentage and the marks, and though she said nothing in front of my father or my sisters, I knew she was too disappointed with me. Pondering about it made me uncomfortable.

Soon the building and the stretch of green ground came in view as she parked the school in front of one of the TISCO worker's house. The whole colony there was constructed for the workers who worked there, and to be honest, I rarely saw any human being come out of the house. I followed her from behind as she led me like she owned the school herself. But the way she walked wasn't arrogant. It was regal, almost like a queen who knew her subjects. The vigilance and the gracefulness in her made her aura colder than ice. I liked it and I wished I would be something like her when I grew up. But I won't scare my kids to death if they weren't able to fulfil what I wanted.

I met many of my classmates on their way back and most of them had pale faces. I was sure about my percentage, but their faces was scaring me to the bones.

The class was soon in view and I dreaded going in but keeping a calm face, I stepped in and sat down on the third bench of the first row beside my mother. The room was empty with only four more students waiting for their faith with their parents. I saw my name on the board chalked in huge capital letters.

TARA SAINI – 1ST (93%)
AARAMBH SINGHANIA – 2ND (89.4%)
VIDISHA KUMARI – 3RD (87.6%)

That percentage pained my eye. I didn't care what others had got (You do, Tara. If it had been someone else in your place with 96%, you'd have committed suicide with this attitude). I didn't even calculate the difference of percentages. That 93% was teasing me. And I *hated* that. *A lot.*

'Here's your report card, and please sign here,' my class teacher smiled and handed the report card to my mother who somehow had a smile on her face too. I didn't check if it was genuine or fake.

'It must be difficult for you to give her time, Mrs. Ruby, but I think your daughter is exceptionally well,' my teacher said. Snow, sitting on the table and looking at my card puffed his chest up, probably in pride. 'At this stage, most of the students fall under the pressure of the sudden change in syllabus, but she has outrun all those things and here she is.'

'I'm truly proud of her, miss,' my mother nodded and I'd to confirm if it was actually my mother speaking. My teacher didn't notice me because Snow was smart enough to remind me I've to not show my emotions like that.

'Don't act like she hated you,' he scolded me. 'She never would. Just scc what happens next.'

Yeah. I'll be dead chicken soon.

After some more praises, we left the school and miraculously, mummy stopped at a café and we sat down in a quiet corner next to a window. We ordered two chocolate pastries and mummy ordered a black coffee for herself. Everything that was happening since the morning had totally left me bizarre. I couldn't process half of the things going on.

She didn't say a word and sipped on her coffee while I took bird bites from the chocolate pastry, sometimes nibbling on the chocolate chips and sometimes, licking the cream clean from the spoon until my buds tasted metal. Was it a way to appreciate my hard work? But I didn't reach her line of expectation. Why was she treating me like a princess?

'Because she's your queen,' Snow said.

The impalpable aura my mother carried around her sure made her the queen of my own fantasy world and myself her youngest and aspiring daughter. But who was to be the next queen would be decided on who was going to take her traits upon growing up. Tarini was like our father; peaceful, sometimes commanding but only when the pressure about the right thing was from someone else. The kind of elder sister with sunlight which was warm for cold days but which would even burn you at times. If mother was the queen of Sun, Moon and Stars, she was the Sun Princess. Ava on the other hand possessed most of the queen's qualities, more of which was grumpiness but no regal grace. She radiated coldness like the winter night, but that term had been saved for me. In short, Ava was the Moon Princess. At last came Tara, the princess the queen cared the most among the three though she loved them all equally, and the princess who was most probably trained much farther than the other two. Though my name meant 'star' when translated to English, I'd a cold nature like winter snowflakes. So most probably I was the Night Winter star. I didn't consider myself a princess but my queen's assassin being trained to assassinate obstacles and achieve excellence in the art.

The question still rose as to who was going to be the next queen; and out of fantasy, it meant who was going to be the able one. I'd literal weird fantasies in myself.

The queen loves her daughters equally. But she loves me less now because I disgraced her with my sexuality and grades.

But all the while I was there, she said nothing. What the purpose of this treat was, I could hardly understand. After we were done, we left the café and she drove me back home to get done with her second half shift of the day. I was sitting in my room dumbfounded.

'All of this is confusing me,' I said to Snow while sitting down to study for a while in the afternoon. 'First she read my diary, and Snow, when I think about it, I believe you were right...'

'About privacy?'

'I'm afraid yes,' I nodded at him. 'I mean, I sure do deserve some privacy after doing so much to keep the heads high. I know mummy should know everything about what I do, but we can have a conversation and she can just try to interact with me more than just peak at my personal stuff.'

'I thought you'd never understand this,' Snow said in actual awe that made me whack him lightly.

'I'm a seventeen year old teenager who'll be a young adult in a few months from now. And I deserve privacy a little bit. Why can't mummy just spend some quality time with me instead of being rude to me all the time? I do study all the time but whenever she enters the room and asks me to focus on the academics rather than wasting time on poetry and writing, which I've left for now because nobody understands my passion for it, I lose all the confidence and I don't even feel like studying at all. And I'm telling you Snow, this treat we had today doesn't make a difference in her attitude towards me. She'll continue reminding me that I've to run and I can't stop to take a breath. Why can't I just take a little bit of breath every day? And you don't know, you'll call me a hypocrite after this statement I'm going to say. I actually don't want to breathe. Because if I'll breathe, I'll only remind myself every second about how worthless I'm becoming. I'm bound to some chains which I'll never be able to break myself from. And mummy never understands that.'

'About my bisexuality, I don't know if I'm right in that because now I can feel my confidence shattering in me. Even though one of my sisters and even Prasanna don't mind that, I feel I'm bringing much more disgrace to my family. I can't ignore the society now because that's where I've to live. I understand it's the God's decision, but I'm not acceptable here. I'll always be a criminal in everybody's mind. In India, that's the harsh reality. There *are* people who aren't homophobic and who support the LGBTQ community even if they are straight, but I wouldn't reveal my sexuality to *everyone* to know who's homophobic and who doesn't mind at all, would I? Why should I be open to people about myself? Only to hear their harsh words about me, if not in front of me, then behind my back? Why should I let go of my secrets if people can't contain it? Sometimes, I think if it was right to tell Prasanna about it, because I know Ava won't do that, but after what all I suffered from my own friends who were only envious and never cared about the efforts I gave in, I've developed trust issues. I never tell anyone about what goes in me, because I fear the same thing will happen over and over again and the loop will never break. I don't want to give chance. Even after years of relationships, people are getting cheated and I get new friends ever year. Nothing lasted forever and it never will do. How can I trust my own friends?'

Snow listened quietly and I continued on.

'Being a valedictorian is not easy. The success, the awards, the achievements they are sweet and I'm proud that I'm one of the valedictorians. The praises are my fuel and it feels like the whole world that appreciates me with vengeance in their eyes, I feel like their idol. You know you're on the top when there's people who are vengeful with you. But behind all of this, we make sure to not show how hollow we become from inside while feeding the title to keep it alive. It might not be the case for everyone, for some are far more excellent while some of us begin to thrive to keep the title with us because we're greedy. Yes I'm greedy for all the praises and the attention. We all are because it's so better. But later on when the load increases like hell, it eats us apart from our hobbies and passion. Some people may find it dramatic, because they think our life is better but it's no better than them. We face many things and when you get the habit of winning, you fear losing and so you become paranoid and give your life at stake. People never see the hard-work but you get even one mark less than someone even if it's only in one subject, the whole class will look at you like *they* didn't expect this from you. Don't give your own notes which you've prepared by keeping awake at night to someone and they'll start spreading rumours that you've become arrogant. For many events they'll just randomly give my name for volunteering even if *I* would've not done that. Teachers expect me to participate in all the programs and then they'll give me the most disgusting look ever, like it was my fault as well. Why do they not understand that I need time to breathe? Oh well, I forgot I can't so I've to work like a fucking robot all the day.'

I took a sip from my steel bottle and looked at Snow casually, who'd frozen like a statue giving a look that he was too realistic to be a statue. Then I poked him in his cheeks and he flinched silently.

'I'm sorry for the long speech but that's what I'd written in my diary, a little too elaborated,' I told him. My mouth muscles hurt a little since I wasn't habitual to talking that much. I opened my books and studied until it was evening. But all the while, I kept thinking about my words. It was the first time I'd actually given vocal life to my thoughts and that too to a magical rabbit. It was much easier to tell him as he was not going to tell about it to anyone. Plus, I wasn't going to cry anymore about it because it'd become my routine. I could only think about these things but there was no end to this. It was a never-ending amnesia. I forgave things, but somehow they struck back to me.

'But you shouldn't have said like that to Neera,' Snow said. 'She never treated you differently. I think you should apologise to her.'

'Whatever,' I snorted. 'It'd be better if I just forget I'd any crushes on her.'

'You won't, and you'll apologise soon,' he showed his teeth to me.

'So you can see the future?' I demanded.

'I don't know.'

'Idiot.'

I felt suffocated so I took some blank papers where I wrote poems and hid in my books and now and then, whenever a teacher took my book to teach a page would always fall down and they'd say, 'Ah! There goes another of her scripts.' I remembered Neera would read each one of my stories and scripts which were never going to be finished or published.

Bound by chains of excellence,

The valedictorians stare out at the night sky of stars
Their hands clasped to books and books and books,
In which they have interest none.
The tittle too big to loose, the head too high to lower,
They're stuck in a forever loop.
They're afraid to loose themselves, if the title is lost,
And identity they wear like one of their masks.
Perhaps it's best if they follow,
The norm that have been set for them
To retain their shadow as always.
A new battle to prepare, a new challenge to face,
They can't narrate the plight they carry
Others think it's easy, others think its best,
When it's only the excellence that tests.
Tell us the cost of this,
Is it your passion bleeding?
Or the forced desire to win the rat race?

'I don't understand why she doesn't let you follow your passion,' Snow said, leaning over the page and sniffing it. I found myself thinking if he could read, and then obviously he could. After all, he could *speak* in our language.

'Maybe because this passion can wriggle in my mind and come in the way of my race,' I smiled at him. 'I'd already made my mind to neither do engineering nor medical. And this pissed my parents too much. So I'm not allowed to do anything apart from studying.'

'That's not even a valid reason, you know,' Snow retorted.

'I can understand this now,' I nodded. 'But this isn't my life.'

Soon, it was time for Tarini and Ava to come and when they burst into the house and caught me in bear hug, I almost choked.

'THE IDOL HAS MADE IT AGAIN!' Tarini shouted in amazement and the complaint boxes outside disguised as neighbourhood aunties looked in. Ava closed the door right when some more peaked in shamelessly. We were sprawled on the floor like three idiots and my sisters grinned at me. I sighed at them.

'Come on, you've managed to be the flawless idol yet again,' Ava rubbed my back gently. 'And for that, we've brought something for you.'

I saw a small plastic in Tarini's hand who was still kneeling on her knees. It had something packed in aluminium packet and soup in another plastic packet. I immediately understood what it was.

'Momos!' she said with glee. 'Only for you. And this will be our little secret.'

'How-But mummy- Wait, why?' I couldn't process it. The image of the corn-flour snack sent danger signals all over my system and I could neither smile at the care of my sisters for me nor thank them.

'Don't worry, eat it up quickly now so that Ava can wash the utensils and keep them in place before she comes,' Tarini said.

'Hey, why is it always me?' Ava snorted at her.

'You can do this for her, she's your sister only,' Tarini snapped at her and rushed into the kitchen. Ava followed behind while I helped my-self up and stared at the doorway as they argued with each other for washing the dishes.

My sisters. The only ones after Neera who thought I was way too perfect than mother's vision of a perfect daughter. I could hardly assess what was going on inside my mind because I was overwhelmed by their pride on me. Not once did they doubt my title and my grades. They were too confident. Confident that I'd never let them down.

'Now what are you doing standing there?' Ava scolded me. 'Go wash your hands.'

I nodded and hopped to the bathroom. When I came back, I saw them serving me and welcoming me like I was some VIP.

'Sit mistress,' Tarini said and I giggled. The smell of momos and their sight made my stomach rumble. I ate and shared with them while giving them each a kiss on their cheeks.

'And here, I've something else for you too,' Ava said, fishing out a small black pouch from her hoodie pocket. She showed it to me while I stuffed another bite in my mouth.

'What's this?' I asked while chewing.

'Given by someone special,' she grinned mischievously. I wondered who it was. But then, her face struck me and I couldn't stop my blush.

'Give it here!' I said and snatched it from her. Tarini looked at us, confused but still smiling.

'You've a boyfriend?' she asked me like it was quite normal for an Indian daughter.

'Apparently, a girlfriend for sure,' Ava told her and I whacked her to shut up. Tarini looked at me as if it was completely normal and smiled.

'Neera isn't it?'

'How do you know?'

'The way you look at her tells everything. And not to hide, I found one of your poems about her.'

'You did WHAT?'

'Now, now, at least, we won't kick your ass out of the house for loving a girl,' Ava said, looking at Tarini, who nodded. I glared at them, but then why was I even hiding it from Tarini? She wasn't homophobic.

'She's not my girlfriend!' I snapped at Ava who couldn't stop laughing.

'You forgot to add "yet",' Tarini said, giggling.

Soon, I finished the momos and after eating them, I felt like a rule-breaker. But eating for one day wasn't going to hurt anyone.

But mummy...

Tarini took us to her room to show something interesting according to her. Unfortunately, I didn't hear the knock on the door, nor did I see Ava wriggle from Tarini's side to open the door. I was too focused on where I shouldn't have been.

When Ava greeted her, I jumped up, scaring Tarini but before I could fly away, she caught my hands.

'Why're you so scared?' she asked, confused.

'I should be studying now!' I squeaked hurriedly and tried to jerk her away. But she wouldn't leave me and she herself pulled me to the living room. There, I saw mother, sitting on the couch and her cold eyes scanned me as I tried to hide behind Tarini like a little kid who'd stolen some chocolates and had been caught.

'You should be studying,' she said coldly.

'We were spending some sister moments, mom,' Ava rolled her eyes and folded her hands, standing beside me. I didn't know if I'd just imagined it for the sake of feeling safe, but they were like a shield in front of me.

'Not when she has the most important exams to prepare for,' mother continued coldly.

'Some minutes won't cut her grades,' Tarini said calmly. 'I don't understand. She's not a machine, ma. Even she needs to have her mind freshened up.'

'If she feels stressed with this level of studies, I can only think her crying all day in the college.'

'Yeah, because you've always made her feel disgraceful for her whole life,' Tarini retorted, holding my hand. 'Not once have you appreciated how hard she works for making *you* proud but you are never satisfied! Even for once the teachers don't act like this but you're too extreme, mom, and that's not good at all!'

'Don't you use that tone on me, young lady,' my mother got up and snarled. I felt like I was being made outcast but my sisters, the Sun Princess and the Moon Princess were guarding me. Protecting me. 'You'll never know how hard one has to work to get into a good college, and this madam here doesn't want to do JEE or NEET which can ultimately get her good packages and the best company!' my mother said sternly.

'We do understand she has to work hard, but according to you, working hard means giving up what you love,' Ava said in a calm tone which was almost impossible for her in an argument with mom. 'And I understand why you never let her write. Because you fear she'll take that up as a career, even when she has plans other than that. The problem is, you don't even listen to her. JEE and NEET can't decide her life mom. She has nothing to do with these two!'

'Don't talk back to me!' my mother shouted, her eyes filled with fury and I only hid behind my sisters. Snow came to me and touched my hand as I tried to hold back the tears.

I'm the cause of this.

'That's how a conversation works!' Ava said but I felt Tarini tug at her sleeves. I didn't look at them. I was behind them with my eyes closed. But the aura of my mother's anger had filled the room entirely. I could feel it peeling my skin slowly.

'This is what you've to give me, Tara?' she yelled. Before I could understand what was happening, my shields were pushed aside and I was held tightly with warm hands that almost broke my wrist. I looked in my mother's eyes but the coldness had suddenly turned to a snowstorm which I couldn't handle. I felt my heart burst inside me. I thought I was going to get nicely on my cheeks but she only looked blackly at me.

'I work for you, I never let you have any discomfort and this is how you treat your mother?' she cried. 'You'll never understand anything about what I do for you!'

'Literal gas-lighting going on here,' Ava muttered under her breath. Over the thunder of my heart which was increasing with each second, I could now barely hear what everyone was saying. I just wanted everything to end. I was wrong. I was wrong with my thoughts. I wish I'd never took out my frustration in front of Snow a few hours ago. This was the fruit I was getting.

Suddenly, she left my hand and I wiped my tear-laden eyes to clear the vision. I saw her duppatta disappear around the bend of my room and chills crept up my spine. I looked at Tarini and Ava who now looked helpless but they wouldn't look at me. I heard rustles from my room and soon, my mother had some of my pages of life in her hands, crumpled under her grip. It already pained me to see the condition of those pages.

'This is what you do, isn't it?' she shouted. 'You won't understand until I take the harsh step!'

And there came the cries of the poems and the words as their vessel was torn slowly. With each tear, my heart cracked inside my chest and the tears stopped. Shock took over when she threw the pieces down at my feet and I fell down to catch them like a lover catching her lover at his last breathe. I held the torn pieces in my hand and looked at the writings. I caught Neera's last words in the lines, which were now destroyed.

I was suddenly angry. No, this was more than being angry; I was *infuriated.* How carefully I'd been planning to write without disrupting my study whenever I felt sad. Those little day dreams about being with Neera, trying to accept myself, praising the little beauties of nature. And now look at this. At *this.* I couldn't control it now. I couldn't harness it anymore. I was *not* wrong. I was being myself. And being yourself had nothing to be wrong.

'I hate you!' I screamed so that she could hear it. My mother was shocked. She'd not expected that from me. And nor was she expecting that I was standing up for myself. 'A good parent doesn't state what they've done for their children! And moreover, they don't *kill* the dreams of their children! It was *your* choice to have a third child! Why didn't you stop yourself then?"

'You don't talk to me like that!' she shouted loudly. But I gathered the pieces in my hands delicately and looked at her with hatred in my heart.

'You've hurt my feelings, mummy,' I said, trying not to break down there. 'You've done what is the greatest sin for a writer and something in which their souls thrive. I may have stopped writing stories in diaries papa gave me but I still have the gift of God and six years of practice with me. You can't take that away from me! YOU CAN'T TAKE MY GIFT!'

She said nothing but inhaled sharply, looking at me with fury eyes.

'And you've invaded my privacy as well, and I believe that is included in chaining your child,' I said, now in a softer voice because I couldn't shout with the lump in my throat. I couldn't find out how the words were just pouring out of my mouth, but I didn't stop them. Now was the time. 'You never talk to me straight way. You say you have no time. But you *do* have time to peak into my diary!'

'SHUT UP!' she screamed so loudly and fumed in anger. But she said nothing and rushed past me into her room. 'I wish I kept you all in boarding schools!'

'That would've given us more reasons to hate you,' Ava muttered but Tarini elbowed her. I picked up the pieces and went into my room without looking at them. Snow followed me and said nothing, as I sat down to study. But of course I couldn't.

I heard a knock at my door. It was open but Tarini and Ava still didn't step inside.

'Are you fine?' Tarini asked and I nodded.

'I need time with myself,' I told them. 'Tarini, would you give me my diary please?'

She nodded and in minutes, I was penning down everything I'd felt in those moments of disaster. That was the end of it. And I knew it.

If being a disgrace removes the chains, I'll be that for the sake of my gift and my life.

7

16ᵗʰ *September 20XX,*

I wonder why my friends have stopped including me in their discussions. Did I do something wrong? But as far as I remember, I did nothing which may have angered them. And why would it anger all of them? Even today, when I tried to be in their group while we were having our break, they kept shifting away to exclude me and I couldn't understand what was happening until Neera pointed that out to me. She scolded me like anything. Said I was being too nice to such people. But I wondered... why did they act like this in the first place? Maybe, the reason is that, I didn't help them with the class notes. Why should I have? It was my hard-work and mummy says that I shouldn't give my hard-work to anyone just to make their work easier. And that's true. I worked hard, why should they enjoy it? I researched each and everything about the topic, spent hours doing so and in the end, they expect me to give them everything as if that's in the pact of friendship. I'm leaving them for sure this time.

**

14ᵗʰ *February 20XX,*

Tanuj revealed to me that he has a crush on me. I mean, why? I thought he was just a friend and I thought I'd such a good friend. Why do boys always have to take everything in the direction of love? At first, I couldn't believe that. I'm just so disgusted by him. Can I get a true friend now? Other than Neera???

5th August 20XX,

I'm the worst daughter ever. I feel Tarini and Ava are better than me. I got 92% in my first term and I've degraded down from 95% which I received in the second term in standard eight. I'm such a disgraceful child. I put in my hundred percent but the test was not checked properly. Mummy has taken away my diaries and she won't give them back. Time limit? Never ending. That was the end of my writing era. I wish I'd put in a little more effort. She said that she would never give them back even if I scored well. What's the point of scoring better then, when I can be a valedictorian with 92%... No! TARA! You shouldn't think like that! It's your fault. You've to be excellent. You can't be average. Otherwise, they'll get ahead of you! How many times do I need to remind you of this? You're so done! I can't remember the last time when mother was actually proud of me. Was that five years ago in grade 5? I've dropped down so much! I hate myself.

26th October 20XX,

Adri read the letter I'd written to Arsheya, telling her about how they all bullied me for no reason at all. For my friends, enjoying life is bunking classes. They don't understand that's not how I enjoy my life. I enjoyed it most when I could write down about my little world and characters freely in the diaries.

But those were taken away only because of my fault. And for me, bunking classes is being a disrespectful child and bringing down my dignity in front of my own eyes. That's what I'd written and she read it while I was busy taking previous year question papers from the library for practice. Like, how dare did she even open my diary? I gave her to only hold it! That girl really doesn't know how to respect boundaries. I don't care now if she leaves me. It was her fault to keep bullying me for this. I'm glad mother was right about her behaviour and I listened to her.

19ᵗʰ December 20XX,

School is closing soon and so has the group divided now. I don't want to be with anyone. Only Neera is my best friend. But here Prasanna came back to me saying she'll try her best to prove her worth to me. I don't care. I don't want anybody. I don't trust anybody.

**

5ᵗʰ May 20XX,

I've a new best friend now! His name is Swastik and he's so cute! He's a jolly boy and he always makes me laugh and he kind of has conquered my mind now... I always keep thinking about him because he has made me so much comfortable with his words. He understands me way better. I'll never leave him. I'll always keep this friendship intact. I won't take wrong steps like I did in the past. And maybe, this will last till our last breath. But mother doesn't know about him much. I'll not tell her now because she doesn't want me to make friends with opposite gender. Maybe, that's the reason I like Neera? I sometimes can't understand myself.

7ᵗʰ October 20XX,

Swastik said that he wanted to end this... I don't understand anything now...

9ᵗʰ November 20XX,

I'm just fed up of everybody. I hate Swastik! I HATE HIM SO MUCH! Why can't I have a normal best friend in my life (excluding Neera)? I hate everything. I hate him so much! Why do people always use me? I hate my title! I hate being a valedictorian!

10ᵗʰ November 20XX,

Mummy just keeps forcing me to tell her what's wrong even if I told her I'll tell her about it later. Like, she wants me to tell her everything there and then and she doesn't care about how I'm feeling or that, I need my personal space. Like, can you just give me some time? She thinks she's right in everything! I hate it so much...

11ᵗʰ November 20XX,

I hate myself.

12ᵗʰ November 20XX,

I've lost interest in everything and this had to happen while I'm in standard twelve. But I feel useless because I've not taken up JEE or NEET so I feel I should be more grateful that I don't have anything to study at all. I should be grateful that mother didn't force me much and just checks over me all the time. I'm so ungrateful. I feel like a failure.

21ˢᵗ November 20XX,

I asked them to not celebrate my birthday but they never listen... I don't even feel like describing what happened because I'm just tired. And I'm just tried with the psychiatrist mummy has put behind me for 'removing' my bisexuality. That'll never happen, but I do know now that I can't hold myself anymore. I hate her. I hate everyone...

22ᴺᵈ November 20XX,
I didn't go to school today. I'm sick. I'm tired.

29ᵗʰ November 20XX,
I'm not okay...

12ᵗʰ December 20XX,
I'd so many intrusive thoughts crowding my mind today while I was staring at the paper cutter kept in front of me. I couldn't believe I wondered how it'd feel like to bleed. I picked it up and examined it for a long time but then something came over and I threw it away. I hate my psychiatrist but I can't misbehave because I don't want that belt treatment again. It hurt like hell. And it wasn't father if you're thinking... The wounds have not healed yet because I got hit on them while I slept off during studying. What could I've done? I'd been studying continuously with only two hours of sleep since five days.

13th December 20XX,

I cut a fine line on my arm and watched the blood. I gave several cuts to remind myself that I've to work harder.

31st December 20XX,

I want to die but I really don't want to. I'm thinking too much.

Save me.

8

I gazed upon at the stars above this time in my dream. A strange kind of relaxation had dawned upon me as I got up and looked around the carnival tents. There were small bunnies who were walking on two legs and those who were no taller than my waist. They had different kinds of clothes on like humans and were the happiest creatures I'd ever seen. I didn't interrupt them and looked at the view. There were stalls of all the things I liked; dark chocolates, key-chains, dragon puppets, black rings, music cassettes of my favourite songs and all the other things. I took a look at each while Snow wandered around with me.

'This is amazing,' I whispered to him. 'I wish I could stay here forever.'

'Do you realise this was the world you created in your story when you were in standard six?' he said, walking with me. There was no noise around in fact, just soft talks like we were in a café. I saw the water reflection above in the maroon lit night with a white moon. I was gaining my memory faster now. It took me a whole year to realise that I'd my own story land as a dream.

'I love this,' I said to him. 'I was so creative. So good...'

I walked towards the end of the carnival and at the gate. But something overwhelming took over me. The guilt of being disgraceful, the way I talked to my mother, the way every sentence turned to an argument, the way I was becoming ungrateful, the way she looked down upon me...

'That's what we expected,' my father says with a disgusting look on his face. 'Where did our raise go wrong? Why are you like this?'

'I can't help it,' I reply, trying not to break down. 'God-'

'Don't bring God's name in this unholy path you've chosen,' my mother slaps me across my face and I almost fall on the table beside the sofa. The right cheek throbs badly, I can taste blood in my mouth. Maybe I'd cut my tongue or something.

'I wish you were never born,' she says and then breaks down.

I made her cry. I hate myself.

'What did I do to get you? I raised you well, took care of you more than your sisters and this is how you reply us back? I wish you were never born in the first place! You're a burden!'

She gets up and goes into her room as I clear my hazy vision while holding my right cheek. Then comes diaries that hit my body and fall down on my feet. She snatches my hand from me and tug me so hard I almost snap my neck.

'Look! The hell you've created. The only reason you can't get a good package and can't be successful in life. What else did you want? You're so ungrateful... And then, this bisexual drama. You weren't expected to become like this Tara'

I look down at the world under me and burst into sobs. Then comes another slap across which makes my trembling legs give way down.

'STOP CRYING!' she yells at me but I could only sob. 'STOP IT!'

I hear the main door open. Tarini rushes in and kneels beside me. Herr faces are pale and drained of colour.

And I drift into unconsciousness.

.

.

.

'I wish we'd never been born in this family.'

.

.

.

'Tara... Tarini di, is she okay?'

'The doctor said she had vasovagal syncope, something which happens when the nervous system overreacts to a trigger, specifically, emotional triggers. I... I wish I was there for her at that time when they were treating her like this... I'm so sorry Tara...'

'Only if we could get her out of that loud house, Tarini. When will we get a job?'

'We can't do that now... Hey, Neera, you can go back to your house now. I don't think you should wait till late here.'

'It's fine, Tarini di. My father and mother allowed me to be here. I'll be with her.'

'I'm not allowing that lady to touch her from now on, Tarini. Mark my words. I didn't know this would stretch on till this!'

'Hush! Don't be too rude. I guess... they're just homophobic. You know how mother's dignity is way more important to her than Tara's happiness. I shouldn't say this but this was the reason I feared becoming the topper.'

'Whatever... I haven't seen people like my parents ever before. Don't ask me to be nice with them Tarini.'

'It's fine Tarini and Ava di, not everyone accepts everyone in this world. And we can't force them to.'

'I just hope Tara is fine. This trauma...'

.

.

.

'Tara, don't give up on hope.'

I began crying. I cried loudly, but nobody looked at me. I cried my eyes out and shouted until my chest hurt and my neck became sore. I screamed until I felt my voice drown. I threw whatever I could find around and fell on my knees banging the ground until I collapsed with sweat all over my body.   Tears soaked the ground beneath me as my hands fell in front of my eyes. The cuts still hadn't faded. They'd become scars. Scars I'll never forget.

'I was wrong at times too. But couldn't it have been solved without slapping me? She was wrong at so many places. But I was the only one wrong in that too. I wish I'd been a little stronger to overcome everything. I don't want to be weak.'

'Crying is never a weakness,' Neera hugs me tightly and kisses me on my forehead. The room is a little dark with only the cloudy light filtering in. 'You've been holding for long. Just let it go.'

I dig my face into her neck and feel the warmth but soon it gets wet with my tears. She strokes my back and hugs me even tighter. They are not home, so it's less of a burden then.

'I'm burden,' I say.

'Hush! Don't say like that. You're not a burden. You're the most perfect idol I've ever seen and I love you for yourself. You're the strongest person I've ever met.'

'*A valedictorian. Such a long word for a worthy position. You know one thing Tara, when we compete, it's not about who's better or who's the best. It should never be that. The only thing you need to remember is that you compete with yourself in this. The race you're running, it's not about your competitors because after your success, nobody's going to ask your percentage when they'll get to know you. They'll surely know you were the valedictorian but they should know you as the valedictorian who fought the battle with herself and not with others. The valedictorian who chased excellence, the valedictorian who contains a vast space of knowledge in her, the valedictorian who was never envious. That's what this word means, and this title means. You're on that path Tara, and you've a long way to walk. Just hold on to hope and fight not with others but with yourself. Make yourself better than your past. And you'll win the battle ultimately.*'

She looked at me gave me a long kiss on my left cheek.

'*As for your bisexuality, not everyone's going to accept that, not here in India. But God made you, and God loves his children. He'll never hate you. And being like this is not a crime. It's the society but what do we have to do with some people who'll spend their entire life taking out follies from your work. Just live your life to the fullest. And know this that Turini, Ava and I are always there for you. At some point, maybe your parents will be too but for now we are here.*'

'*And I'm here too Tara,*' *Snow grinned and I smiled.*

Snow was in front of me as I got up, feeling dizzy. In front of me I saw the same road, the same setting, but no traffic this time. I blinked at it several times and then looked at Ambience, wiping my running nose and eyes. Without wasting further time, I ran over to her and stopped abruptly in front of her. She craned her neck to look down.

She was glowing, Ambience was glowing.

'I'm you,' she said in a voice similar to mine. 'And you've already won half the battle. Keep going and fly with me.'

'I will,' I nodded at her. Ambience let down her neck and I hugged her.

I had nothing to worry about now. It was me and myself. And the battle was mine. I was going to be the perfect idol for myself. I knew I'd embarked on a new journey, the one which will be of my own will. And for the first time, tears of *happiness* slid down my cheeks.